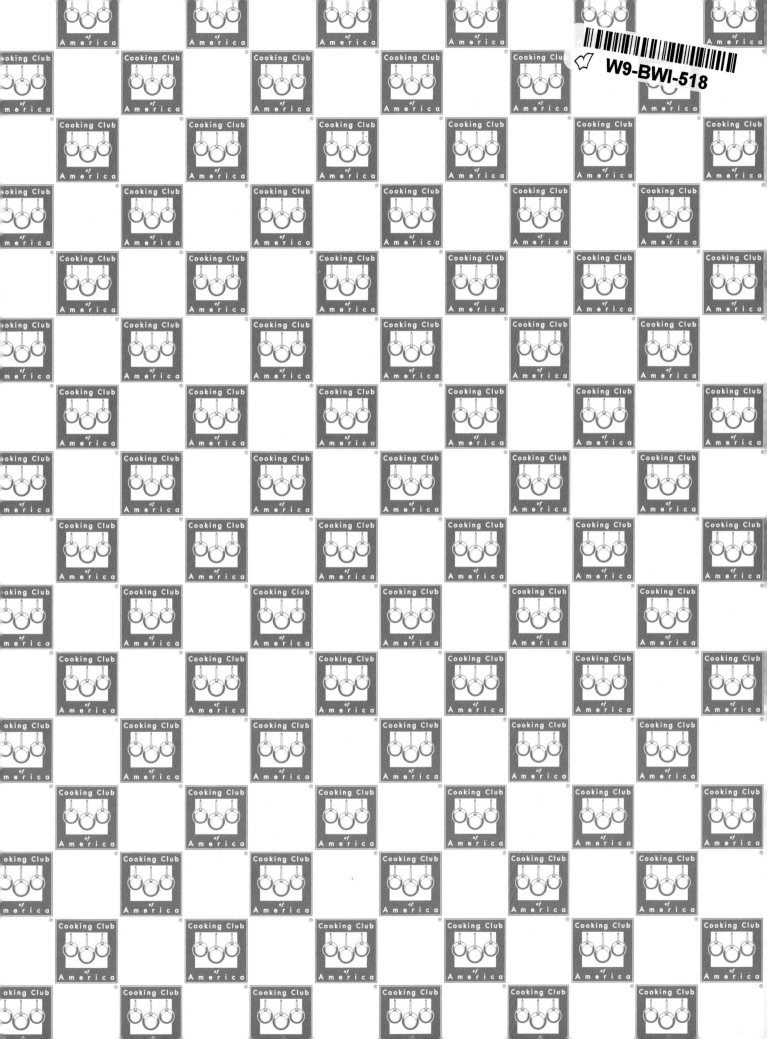

IT'S ALL ABOUT
DESSERT

Cooking Arts Collection™

CREDITS

IT'S ALL ABOUT DESSERT

Printed in 2006.

Tom Carpenter, Creative Director
Jennifer Guinea, Senior Book Development Coordinator
Jenya Prosmitsky, Book Design
Gina Germ, Book Production
Laura Holle, Senior Book Development Assistant
Phil Aarrestad Photography, Commissioned Photography
Robin Krause, Cindy Ojczyk, Food Stylists
Susan Telleen, Assistant Food Stylists
Robin Krause, Prop Stylist

Special Thanks to: Terry Casey, Walter Chandoha, Elizabeth Gunderson, John Keenan, Cindy Jurgensen, Bea Krinke, Mary Jo Myers, Ruth Petran and Martha Zeimer.

5 6 7 8 9 10 / 10 09 08 07 06
©2002 Cooking Club of America
ISBN 1-58159-167-5

On Cover: Pumpkin Swirl Cheesecake, page 48.
On Page 1: Individual Apple Tarts, page 159.

Cooking Club of America
12301 Whitewater Drive
Minnetonka, MN 55343
www.cookingclub.com

Maple Date Bars, page 20

Gingered Carrot Spice Cake, page 35

Apple Cream Cheese Bars, page 51

$\mathcal{T}$ABLE OF CONTENTS

Coconut Tea Cakes, page 71

Mousse Au Chocolate, page 89

Pumpkin Pots de Crème, page 110

*I*NTRODUCTION

Culinary passions run deep.

Appetizers are great, easing things into motion (or keeping a party going) with wonderful little taste-filled notes. Soups make for warm preludes. Salads are good for you, and they add light and refreshing harmony. Of course, superb main dishes become the melody of any meal — the center around which everything else revolves. Side dishes add necessary and pleasing variety.

But what really matters in the symphony of food? Dessert! True, dessert doesn't usually offer extensive nutrient value. But, for those of us who love dessert (and who doesn't, in one form or another), it stirs a passion deeper than any other kind of food.

Let's be honest. When we were little kids and the world was about fun, eating was about dessert. Yes, we've learned to eat right, and to appreciate other fine tastes. But in the end, still, *It's All About Dessert*.

That's why we created this book especially for Cooking Club of America members, and named it what we named it: Dessert truly is food for the soul, and these pages cover the topic, start to finish, top to bottom, inside and out, first note to final flourish.

You'll find over 100 recipes in all here: brownies & bars, cakes, cheesecakes, cookies, custards & mousses & puddings, fruit desserts, fudges & candy, ice creams & other frozen delights, pastries & tarts, and of course, pies.

To pull each theme together even more completely, each chapter features

an introductory "essentials" section that immerses you in a crash course on that kind of dessert or treat. You'll understand the ingredients you'll need, learn important terms, master necessary techniques, discover specific tools to have on hand, and get plenty of tips and insights that will make creating dessert both successful and rewarding.

To bring you even more complete and honest insight, each chapter was prepared by a different cooking pro immersed in that topic.

It is true that humankind does not live by dessert alone. In fact, we could probably live without it. But would life be as good?

That's why, in the end, we knew the truth had to be told: *It's All About Dessert.*

BARS & BROWNIES

by Connie Hay

Not quite cake but certainly not cookies ... bars and brownies have carved their own wonderful niche in the world of desserts. Here are some classic, updated and all-new ideas to call your own.

Coconut-Capped Brownies, page 12

No one seems to know when and how brownie recipes originated. A recipe called "Brownies" appeared in the cake section of the 1896 edition of The Boston Cooking-School Cookbook. *They were flavored with molasses and pecans, which would account for a brown appearance, but they did not contain chocolate, which was not yet a common ingredient except in cocoa and hot chocolate.*

By the early 20th century, recipes we would later recognize as brownies appeared in two Boston cookbooks. The first appeared in the 1906 edition of The Boston Cooking-School Cookbook *and others soon followed in the 1907 edition of* Lowney's Cookbook, *published by a local chocolate distributor.*

Once the idea of using unsweetened chocolate in baked goods took hold, it wasn't long before creative cooks worked their magic with embellishments for other brownies and bars.

Brownies fall somewhere between a cookie and a cake. They are often categorized by whether they are chewy or cake-like, and sometimes by their fudginess. We love them for their infinite variety whether they are chocolate or blonde, as the non-chocolate varieties are dubbed.

INGREDIENTS

As with any recipe, it's best to read it thoroughly, gather all the ingredients, and measure them before proceeding so that nothing is omitted by mistake. One of the joys of making bars and brownies is that many of them call for ingredients that may already be staples in your kitchen.

BUTTER. Professional bakers prefer unsalted butter, but you can use salted butter and then reduce or eliminate the amount of salt. Remove butter from the refrigerator about 30 minutes before using to allow it to become "softened" in recipe terminology. Do not substitute whipped or reduced-calorie butter.

CHOCOLATE. Baking chocolate is available in bittersweet, unsweetened and semisweet varieties, usually wrapped separately in one-ounce portions. Chocolate chips are available in mini and regular size and in milk chocolate, semisweet and mint. Semi-sweet chunks are also available and save the cook an extra knife step.

Be very careful when melting chocolate, as it is easily scorched. Melt it over low heat, watching carefully and stirring occasionally. If you prefer to use the microwave, follow the directions on the package, but generally use 50% power for 1 minute and stir the chocolate. Repeat once. If it is not completely melted, try once again for 30 seconds at 50% power or simply allow it to stand a few minutes and let the residual heat complete the job.

CANDIED FRUIT. Cherries, pineapple, citrus rinds or a combination called "mixed fruits" are prepared in sugar syrup and sold for use in baked goods and candies. Usually available in supermarkets during the fall for fruitcake and other Christmas baking, candied fruit may be more elusive at other times of the year. It's smart to purchase a little extra to have on hand. Store it in an airtight container in a cool, dry place. In gourmet or specialty shops, candied fruits may be called glacé fruits.

DRIED FRUITS. Apricots, blueberries, cherries, dates and raisins are just a few of the dehydrated fruits commonly used in baking. Nearly 75% to 85% of the moisture is removed from the fresh fruit, resulting in more intense flavor and sweetness. Available year 'round, many dried fruits are now packaged with a self-closing seal which helps keep them fresh for up to 12 months.

EGGS. The recipes to come were tested with large eggs unless otherwise noted. Larger or smaller eggs may result in too much or too little liquid, which may affect baking timing and final results. Bring eggs to room temperature before using.

EXTRACTS AND FLAVORINGS. Always purchase pure almond, orange or vanilla extracts, not imitations. The intense flavor is well worth the additional cost, and a properly stored bottle will last a long time.

FLOUR. Use all-purpose flour, either bleached or unbleached, to prepare brownies and bars. Flour needn't be sifted — just stir it well, lightly spoon it into a measuring cup, and level with the edge of a knife or small metal spatula.

SPICES. Cinnamon, cardamom, cloves and nutmeg are common spices used in baking. Initially they may seem expensive, but the special aroma and flavor they impart are well worth the price. Store in a cool, dry place and they will keep for over a year.

NUTS. Nuts add wonderful texture and flavor to brownies and bars. Pecans, walnuts and almonds are longtime American favorites. Hazelnuts (also called filberts) and pine nuts (called *pignoli* or *piñons* in ethnic markets) are now commonly available.

SUGAR. Brownie recipes may call for granulated, light brown or dark brown sugars depending on the desired flavor profile. Brown sugars contain molasses. Light brown sugar has a delicate flavor, while dark brown sugar has a more pronounced molasses flavor. Molasses contributes to brown sugar's fluffy texture; always measure it by firmly packing it into a measuring cup. Powdered sugar, or confectioners' sugar, is granulated sugar processed into a powder form that dissolves quickly. This is especially useful in candy and icings. For a smooth result, sift powdered sugar to prevent lumps.

One of the reasons brownies and bars are so popular is that they do not require special kitchen equipment. You can prepare many basic brownie and bar recipes entirely by hand in a heavy gauge saucepan — from melting the butter and sugar or chocolate to combining the rest of the ingredients. Just be careful to let the hot ingredients cool before continuing. Then swiftly scrape the batter into a prepared baking pan. No mess, no muss, no fuss!

BAKING PANS. An 8-inch square aluminum or Pyrex pan is most commonly used. Remember when using Pyrex, reduce the baking temperature by 25 degrees.

Use the specified size baking pan. Otherwise the timing and texture of the finished project will be off. If you don't own a 15x10x1-inch pan, you may substitute 2 (9x9x2-inch) pans.

MEASURING CUPS. There are two types of measuring cups, dry and liquid. Dry measures are those sold in sets from ¼ cup up to 1 cup. They are designed to give accurate measure when the dry ingredient is slightly overfilled, then leveled with the side of a knife or spatula. Liquid measures are generally made of Pyrex, with measurements on the side, a pouring spout, and extra top space so the liquid does not overflow. To read accurately, place the cup on a level surface and read at eye level.

MIXERS. Most brownie and bar recipes do not require an electric mixer. But some icings benefit from the consistent speed of a hand mixer. Only the *Chocolate Spice Bars* (page 18) batter is so thick that it requires a heavy stand mixer or well-toned arms and plenty of "elbow grease."

RUBBER SPATULAS. Rubber spatulas or scrapers make quick work of thick brownie and bar batters. New types made of silicone are impervious to color changes from chocolate and other foods which stain.

WAX PAPER, PARCHMENT AND FOIL. Line your baking pans with wax paper, parchment paper or aluminum foil extended over the edges of the pan for easy clean-up and removal of the baked product. Spray the paper with nonstick cooking spray or grease with butter or shortening.

WHISK. Thoroughly combine the dry ingredients with a whisk to avoid the bitter taste that sometimes occurs when baking powder or soda clumps together.

WIRE COOLING RACKS. Remove the hot baking pan from the oven and immediately place it on a wire cooling rack. Cool to room temperature before cutting the brownies or bars.

TERMS & TECHNIQUES

Busy cooks love to fix brownies and bars because they require no special techniques. They are quicker to bake than batches of cookies, with no constant trips to the oven, and no re-washing cookie sheets and refilling them repeatedly with fresh mounds of cookie dough. Once the pan of brownies or bars goes into the oven, the cook's job is nearly done

TEST. Learning to recognize when brownies are done is the most difficult part of making them. Always set the timer to bake for the *minimum* amount of time recommended. Test with a toothpick about halfway there between the center and the rim of the pan. A moist crumb indicates the brownies are ready. Do not over-bake. Another indication that the brownies are ready is that the batter starts to pull away from the sides of the pan. Place the pan on a wire rack and cool thoroughly.

STORAGE. Most brownies and bars freeze well in aluminum foil or plastic storage bags for up to one month. They also keep well for several days in tins, separated into layers with parchment paper.

TIPS AND INSIGHTS

Brownies are one of the most popular dessert and snack items around. Follow these tips and insights for success every time.

- FOR FUN IN THE KITCHEN WITH KIDS, CUT THE BARS OR BROWNIES INTO INTERESTING SHAPES. Use diamond, heart, circle, star or animal cookie cutters to turn ordinary bars and brownies into memorable treats.

- COOL BARS OR BROWNIES IN THE PAN BEFORE SERVING. Cooling the bars or brownies in the pan prevents them from crumbling. Another tip: remove the corner bar or brownie first.

- USE THE PROPER PAN SIZE. And always read the recipe in its entirety before beginning. It also helps to measure ingredients and gather tools before-hand to avoid surprises.

COCONUT-CAPPED BROWNIES

These dainty two-bite brownies are perfect for a fancy occasion, such as an afternoon tea. These brownies are also pictured on pages 6-7.

BROWNIES
- 6 tablespoons butter
- 6 oz. semisweet chocolate chips
- 1 cup sugar
- 2½ cups all-purpose flour
- 2 tablespoons unsweetened cocoa
- ¼ teaspoon baking powder
- ¼ teaspoon salt
- 3 eggs
- 2 teaspoons vanilla

TOPPING
- ⅔ cup sweetened condensed milk
- 2 cups shredded coconut

❶ Heat oven to 350°F. Spray baking sheet with nonstick cooking spray.

❷ In small saucepan, melt butter, chocolate chips and sugar over low heat, stirring occasionally until smooth.

❸ In large bowl, combine flour, cocoa, baking powder and salt; whisk together until well blended. Beat in eggs and vanilla; stir in chocolate mixture. Refrigerate dough 1 hour.

❹ For coconut topping, in medium bowl, combine sweetened condensed milk and coconut; mix well. Cover; refrigerate until brownie dough is firm.

❺ To assemble, using #40 cookie scoop, measure out brownie dough; arrange 2 inches apart on baking sheet. "Cap" each brownie with scoop of coconut mixture using #100 cookie scoop (or use 1 tablespoon for brownie dough and 1 teaspoon for coconut mixture.) Bake 15 to 17 minutes or until brownies are done and coconut is golden.

About 2½ dozen brownies.

Preparation time: 15 minutes. Ready to serve: 1 hour, 20 minutes.

Per serving: 185 calories, 9 g total fat (6.5 g saturated fat), 30 mg cholesterol, 60 mg sodium, 1.5 g fiber.

CHUNKY CHOCOLATE RAISIN BARS

Chocolate-covered raisin lovers will become addicted to the taste of these brownies and their similar sweet, chocolaty aura.

⅔ cup butter
2 cups packed brown sugar
3 eggs
1 teaspoon vanilla
2⅔ cups all-purpose flour
2½ teaspoons baking powder
1 teaspoon ground cinnamon
½ teaspoon salt
1 cup raisins
1 cup semisweet chocolate chunk

1. Heat oven to 325°F. Spray 15x10x1-inch pan with nonstick cooking spray.

2. In medium saucepan, melt butter and brown sugar over medium heat, stirring occasionally. Remove from heat; cool to room temperature. Beat in eggs, one at a time, and vanilla.

3. In large bowl, combine flour, baking powder, cinnamon and salt; mix thoroughly. Combine with brown sugar mixture; stir in raisins and chocolate chunks.

4. Pour mixture into pan. Bake 25 to 30 minutes or until edges are set. Cut into 2-inch squares.

About 3 dozen bars.

Preparation time: 10 minutes. Ready to serve: 2 hours.

Per serving: 150 calories, 5.5 g total fat (3 g saturated fat), 30 mg cholesterol, 100 mg sodium, 0 g fiber.

LAYERED DOUBLE CHOCOLATE-ORANGE BROWNIES

These moist brownies are made with two different kinds of chocolate, then frosted in complementary orange. Topped with another layer of chocolate, these delights are sinfully rich ... and fancy enough to serve to company.

BROWNIES

- 2 (1-oz.) squares unsweetened chocolate
- 1 cup sugar
- 3/4 cup all-purpose flour
- 1/2 teaspoon baking powder
- 1/2 teaspoon salt
- 1/2 cup vegetable oil
- 2 eggs
- 1/4 teaspoon orange extract
- 3/4 cup semisweet chocolate chips
- 1/2 cup chopped walnuts

FROSTING

- 2 cups powdered sugar, sifted
- 1/4 cup (1/2 stick) butter, softened
- 2 tablespoons Cointreau or other orange liqueur
- 1 tablespoon orange juice concentrate
- 2 teaspoons finely shredded orange peel

TOPPING

- 3/4 cup semisweet chocolate chips
- 1/4 cup (1/2 stick) butter

❶ Heat oven to 350°F. Spray 8-inch square pan with nonstick cooking spray.

❷ In small saucepan, heat chocolate over low heat until melted; set aside.

❸ In large bowl, combine sugar, flour, baking powder and salt; whisk well. Mix in oil, eggs, melted chocolate and orange extract. Stir in 3/4 cup chocolate chips and walnuts. Pour into pan. Bake 25 to 30 minutes or just until brownies start to pull away from sides of pan. Cool completely on wire rack.

❹ In another large bowl, combine powdered sugar, 1/4 cup butter, liqueur, orange juice concentrate and orange peel; mix until smooth. Spread frosting mixture over cooled brownies. Refrigerate.

❺ Meanwhile, in small saucepan, heat 3/4 cup chocolate chips and 1/4 cup butter over low heat until melted. Remove from heat; cool. Remove brownies from refrigerator; pour topping over frosting. Return to refrigerator until chocolate is set. Cut into small squares.

16 brownies.

Preparation time: 12 minutes. Ready to serve: 2 hours.

Per serving: 375 calories, 22 g total fat (9 g saturated fat), 40 mg cholesterol, 135 mg sodium, 2 g fiber.

MAPLE DATE BARS

A cake-type bar studded with dates, thick maple frosting further enhances the light maple flavor of these little pieces of perfection.

BARS

1½	cups packed brown sugar
⅔	cup softened unsalted butter
2	eggs
¼	cup milk
1	teaspoon maple extract
2	cups all-purpose flour
1	teaspoon baking soda
1	teaspoon ground cinnamon
½	teaspoon salt
½	teaspoon ground nutmeg
1	cup chopped dates
1	cup chopped pecans

FROSTING

4	cups powdered sugar, sifted
¼	cup (½ stick) unsalted butter, softened
⅓	cup maple syrup
¼	cup milk
½	teaspoon maple extract
½	teaspoon salt
	Pecan halves (optional)

❶ Heat oven to 350°F. Spray 15x10x1-inch pan with nonstick cooking spray.

❷ In large bowl, beat brown sugar and ⅔ cup butter until light and fluffy; beat in eggs, ¼ cup milk and ½ teaspoon maple extract, blending well.

❸ In medium bowl, combine flour, baking soda, cinnamon, ½ teaspoon salt and nutmeg; whisk thoroughly. Beat into brown sugar mixture; stir in dates and chopped pecans. Pour into pan. Bake 25 to 30 minutes or until edges are golden brown. Cool on wire rack.

❹ To make Frosting: In separate large bowl, combine powdered sugar, ¼ cup butter, maple syrup, ¼ cup milk, ½ teaspoon maple extract and ½ teaspoon salt; mix until well blended and smooth. Spread over cooled bars. Cut into squares, then in half to form triangles. Decorate with pecan halves, if desired.

About 3 dozen bars.

Preparation time: 15 minutes. Ready to serve: 1 hour, 40 minutes.

Per serving: 200 calories, 7.5 g total fat (3.5 g saturated fat), 25 mg cholesterol, 110 mg sodium, 1 g fiber.

APRICOT LATTICE BARS

Kids love to help prepare these bars! Let children press the dough into the sheet pan, spread the filling over the base and roll the ropes of extra dough to form the lattice design on top. Don't worry if everything's not letter perfect; this dough is made to be handled.

FILLING

1   (6-oz.) pkg. dried apricots
    Juice of ½ a lemon
1   cup water
¼   to ½ cup sugar or to taste

DOUGH

3   cups all-purpose flour
1   cup (2 sticks) unsalted butter, softened
1   cup sugar
2   eggs
1   teaspoon ground cinnamon
1   teaspoon ground nutmeg
½   teaspoon ground cloves
¼   teaspoon salt
⅓   cup chopped or sliced almonds (optional)

❶ Heat oven to 375°F. Spray 15x10x1-inch baking pan with nonstick cooking spray.

❷ In large saucepan, combine apricots, lemon juice and water; bring to a boil. Cook, covered, over low heat 15 minutes. Stir in sugar to taste; simmer, uncovered, 5 minutes or until slightly thickened. Cool; process in blender or food processor until smooth.

❸ Meanwhile, in large bowl, thoroughly mix flour, butter, 1 cup sugar, eggs, cinnamon, nutmeg, cloves and salt. Press ¾ of dough evenly into pan. Spread filling evenly over dough.

❹ Roll remaining ¼ of dough into free-form ropes; form "lattice" over fruit filling. Lay ropes on diagonal in one direction, then cross in opposite direction. If dough is too soft, roll it in a little extra flour. Ropes do not have to be perfect to make a pretty lattice. If long ropes break, just pinch together over filling or refrigerate dough until it is easier to handle.

❺ Sprinkle nuts over filling, if desired. Bake 30 to 35 minutes or until golden. Cut into rectangles when cooled slightly.

25 bars.

Preparation time: 45 minutes. Ready to serve: 2 hours, 5 minutes.

Per serving: 180 calories, 8 g total fat (5 g saturated fat), 35 mg cholesterol, 30 mg sodium, 1 g fiber.

CHOCOLATE SPICE BARS

Reminiscent of German Christmas cookies sold at the Nuremberg Christkindlmarkt, this dense bar is redolent of spices and filled with candied fruit and nuts. Storing the bars in tins helps the flavors meld, and improves the bars' overall taste with time.

BARS

1½ cups all-purpose flour
1 teaspoon each ground cinnamon, ground cardamom
½ teaspoon each ground cloves, baking powder, baking soda
¾ cup sugar
½ cup honey
4 (1-oz.) squares unsweetened chocolate
3 tablespoons orange juice concentrate
½ cup each blanched almonds, mixed candied fruit
1 egg

CRACKLED GLAZE

½ cup powdered sugar, sifted
2 teaspoons hot water
¼ teaspoon almond extract
Slivered almonds and candied cherries for decorations (optional)

❶ Three hours to 2 days before baking, sift together flour, cinnamon, cardamom, cloves, baking powder and baking soda; set aside.

❷ In saucepan, heat sugar, honey, chocolate and orange juice concentrate over low heat, stirring until chocolate melts; set aside to cool.

❸ In food processor, finely chop almonds and candied fruit. (If too sticky, add 1 tablespoon sugar.)

❹ In large bowl of electric mixer, combine chocolate mixture, nut mixture and egg. Add dry ingredients; mix thoroughly. Cover tightly with aluminum foil; refrigerate 3 hours or up to 2 days to allow flavors to blend.

❺ When ready to bake, bring mixture to room temperature. Heat oven to 325°F; spray 8-inch square pan with nonstick cooking spray. Spread batter into pan. Bake 30 to 35 minutes.

❻ In small bowl, combine powdered sugar, hot water and almond extract. Brush tops of slightly warm bars with glaze. Immediately decorate with almonds and cherries, if desired. Cut into rectangles. Store in tins.

18 bars.

Preparation time: 10 minutes. Ready to serve: 6 hours, 30 minutes.

BLACK FOREST BROWNIES

These brownies are much quicker to make than the famous cake from Germany's Black Forest, but they still capture the flavor.

⅓ cup chopped hazelnuts
⅓ cup butter
2 (1-oz.) squares unsweetened chocolate
1 cup sugar
¾ cup all-purpose flour
½ teaspoon baking powder
½ teaspoon salt
2 eggs
½ teaspoon almond extract
½ cup dried cherries
   Whipped cream (optional)
   Chocolate Curls (optional)

1. Heat oven to 350°F. Spray 8-inch baking pan with nonstick cooking spray.

2. Spread hazelnuts on baking sheet; bake 5 to 7 minutes, stirring once. Remove when golden.

3. In medium saucepan, melt butter and chocolate over low heat until melted; stir in sugar. Set aside to cool.

4. In small bowl, whisk together flour, baking powder and salt until well blended. Stir eggs and almond extract into cooled chocolate mixture; add flour mixture, stirring just until blended. Add hazelnuts and cherries. Pour mixture into pan.

5. Bake 25 to 30 minutes or until set. Cool completely. Cut in wedges. Serve with dollop of whipped cream garnished with chocolate curls, if desired.

16 brownies.

Preparation time: 20 minutes. Ready to serve: 2 hours.

Per serving: 160 calories, 8 g total fat (4g saturated fat), 35 mg cholesterol, 120 mg sodium, 1 g fiber.

PINE NUT BROWN SUGAR BARS

These golden brown bars taste of brown sugar and a hint of cinnamon. An unexpected topping of delicate pine nuts adds the crowning touch.

¼ cup (½ stick) butter
1 cup packed dark brown sugar
1 egg, beaten
1 teaspoon vanilla
1 cup all-purpose flour
1 teaspoon baking powder
½ teaspoon salt
½ teaspoon ground cinnamon
⅔ cup pine nuts

① Heat oven to 325°F. Spray 8-inch square pan with nonstick cooking spray.

② In saucepan, melt butter over medium heat. Remove pan from heat; stir in brown sugar. Let cool; stir in egg and vanilla.

③ In small bowl, combine flour, baking powder, salt and cinnamon; stir into brown sugar mixture, mixing well.

④ Pour mixture into prepared pan. Sprinkle pine nuts evenly over batter. Press nuts lightly into batter.

⑤ Bake 25 to 30 minutes or just until brownies begin to pull away from sides of pan. Cool in pan on wire rack. Cut into bars 2½-inch by 1½-inch.

15 bars.

Preparation time: 15 minutes. Ready to serve: 1 hour, 30 minutes.

Per serving: 150 calories, 7 g total fat (2.5 g saturated fat), 20 mg cholesterol, 145 mg sodium, 1 g fiber.

PRALINE CHEESECAKE SQUARES

These tasty squares, sprinkled with crunchy homemade praline, will tempt the palate of any and every cheesecake lover.

CRUST
- 1 cup all-purpose flour
- ½ cup (1 stick) butter, softened
- ½ cup packed brown sugar

FILLING
- 1 (8-oz.) pkg. cream cheese, softened
- 6 tablespoons sugar
- 1 egg
- ½ teaspoon almond extract
- 1 (12-oz.) carton sour cream

PRALINE
- ½ cup sugar
- ½ cup chopped pecans

1. Heat oven to 350°F. In food processor, process flour, butter and brown sugar just until it forms a ball. Press dough into bottom of 8-inch square pan. Bake 12 to 15 minutes or until golden; cool.

2. In large bowl, beat cream cheese and 6 tablespoons sugar until smooth. Beat in egg and almond extract. Stir in sour cream. Pour into cooled crust. Bake 30 minutes or just until set. Chill; serve sprinkled with praline pieces.

3. To make praline: Line baking sheet with aluminum foil; set aside. In heavy saucepan, cook ½ cup sugar over medium-high heat, shaking pan occasionally, until sugar begins to melt. Do not stir. Reduce heat to low; add pecans. Cook about 3 minutes or until sugar is golden brown and pecans are toasted, stirring occasionally.

4. Carefully pour hot mixture onto foil, spreading as thinly as possible with wooden spoon. Cool completely. Break or chop cooled praline into ¼-inch pieces. Use to decorate desserts or ice cream. Store extra praline in airtight container in refrigerator.

16 squares.

Preparation time: 15 minutes. Ready to serve: 3 hours, 20 minutes.

Per serving: 270 calories, 17.5 g total fat (9.5 g saturated fat), 60 mg cholesterol, 95 mg sodium, .5 g fiber.

PEANUT BUTTER, JELLY AND GRANOLA SWIRL BARS

Children of all ages enjoy the taste of peanut butter and jelly. So for the kid in all of us, here's a brownie with those classic flavors and a bit of granola thrown in, to add an unexpected crunch.

½ cup (1 stick) butter
½ cup sugar
½ cup packed light brown sugar
½ cup creamy peanut butter
1 egg
¼ cup milk
1 teaspoon vanilla
1¼ cups all-purpose flour
½ teaspoon baking soda
½ teaspoon salt
½ cup granola cereal
½ cup grape jelly or favorite flavor jelly or preserves

1. Heat oven to 350°F. Spray 8-inch square pan with nonstick cooking spray.

2. In large saucepan, heat butter over medium heat until melted; remove from heat. Beat in sugar, brown sugar and peanut butter. Stir in egg, milk and vanilla.

3. In medium bowl, combine flour, baking soda and salt; whisk well. Stir dry ingredients into saucepan until blended; mix in granola. Pour into pan. Swirl jelly throughout batter. Bake about 25 minutes or until center is set. Cool on wire rack. Cut into squares.

16 bars.

Preparation time: 15 minutes. Ready to serve: 1 hour, 45 minutes.

Per serving: 230 calories, 10 g total fat (5 g saturated fat), 30 mg cholesterol, 200 mg sodium, 1 g fiber.

CAKES

Forget about the cake mix aisle in the grocery store. Those mere imitations cannot compare with the flavor, variety and excitement you get with a "from scratch" cake like the ones you'll find here. Cake baking is part art, yes, but we'll show you the secrets.

Strawberry Cream Jelly Roll, page 30

ESSENTIALS — CAKES

Cakes signify happy occasions — birthdays, anniversaries and weddings — as well as quiet, everyday living. When I grew up, cakes were an "end of the week" treat that we enjoyed Saturday night and Sunday. It was usually gone by Monday morning! A delicious, made-from-scratch cake was always part of birthday celebrations, and the cakes varied season to season. In the spring when strawberries were plump and juicy, they filled an eggy sponge cake. In the fall, fresh apples and nuts found their way into a cake. And, in the winter we would layer the cakes with bananas or homemade berry preserves and whipped cream.

Here are ten cakes, each of which is simple to make and comes with character, delicious flavor and texture that you can get only from a "scratch" cake. Some of them are old time classics with a new twist, like the Banana Blitz Torte (page 38), *layered with a meringue and filled with fresh bananas. The old fashioned* Apple Date Pecan Cake with Caramel Sauce (page 32) *makes a perfect autumn dessert. Lavish* Flourless Chocolate Grand Marnier Cake (page 41) *graces the menus of the fanciest restaurants, but is incredibly simple to make with just a few ingredients.*

INGREDIENTS

Use the freshest ingredients for the best results. Check expiration dates on everything and discard anything that has been in your cupboard past that date. Before you begin mixing a cake, measure all the ingredients, or at least have them at your fingertips, and bring them to room temperature so that they will be easily incorporated into the batter. Whipping cream is an exception; when it is used for a topping or filling, it needs to be chilled for best results.

EGGS. These recipes were tested using large eggs. Use the freshest possible eggs. Discard any eggs that are cracked or broken in the container. Keep eggs stored in the refrigerator. To quickly bring eggs to "room temperature," place them into a bowl of warm water for a minute or two.

FATS AND OILS. Butter — either salted or unsalted — gives the best result for most cakes. There is a little less than 1/8 teaspoon salt in each stick of salted butter, which may affect the salt level of the cake. Recipes in this collection were tested with lightly salted butter. Cakes that call for oil were tested with a high quality, fresh vegetable oil.

FLOUR. All-purpose flour — a blend of hard and soft wheats — is fine for most cakes. Cake flour is finely milled soft wheat, and should be used in lighter, more tender cakes. In each recipe, the flour that is called for is the flour that the recipe was tested with.

LEAVENING. Both baking powder and baking soda help cakes rise by producing carbon dioxide bubbles. These leavening agents are often used together in a recipe. If baking soda is used in a recipe, there must also be an acid ingredient (such as buttermilk, yogurt or sour cream) to react with the soda to produce bubbles. Baking powder contains both acid and base, which activate when the baking powder is moistened.

SUGARS. Use granulated sugar in cakes, although fast-dissolving superfine or "bakers" sugar can also be used. Brown sugar has molasses added for flavor. It may be dark brown or light brown. Pack brown sugar into the measuring cup for accuracy, and level the top off. Powdered sugar or confectioners' sugar is a very finely ground and sifted sugar; it is most often used when a fine texture is desired, and also in uncooked frostings.

TOOLS

When shopping for cake pans, buy the highest-quality pans you can find and they will last a lifetime. Look for heavy-gauge aluminum pans with well-sealed seams. Cheap pans tend to be thin, and they often get misshapen in the oven. They also have a tendency to discolor or rust. A nonstick surface is useful on some bakeware, such as Bundt and tube pans, but for layer pans such a finish is not necessary.

SPRINGFORM CAKE PANS. These pans have a removable side that closes tightly with a clasp. One 10-inch pan is sufficient, although many seasoned bakers like to have a range of sizes. Rectangular cake pans, 13x9-inch in size, have a variety of uses and may be either glass or metal.

LAYER CAKE PANS. Get both round and square pans, in 8- and 9-inch sizes. You'll need at least two round layer cake pans of each size, three if you make 3-layer cakes. One 8-inch and one 9-inch square cake pan is sufficient.

LOAF PANS. Use these for baking pound cakes. You can also bake Bundt cakes in two 9x5-inch loaf pans.

JELLY ROLL PANS. These are most commonly 15x10x1-inch, ½ to ¾ inches deep, and used for baking thin sheet cakes that roll up to enclose a filling. Sometimes jelly roll pans are called "cookie sheets."

TUBE PAN. A standard tube pan is ten inches in diameter for baking chiffon, sponge and angel-food cakes. Tube pans are available with removable sides, which make it easier to remove delicate cakes from the pan. Fancy tube type pans, such as Bundt pans, have fluted sides and come in a variety of designs. Sizes range from 10-cup to 12-cup capacities.

The goal in mixing cake batter is to have a well-blended emulsion with evenly distributed ingredients surrounded by tiny air bubbles. There are different terms used for each of these mixing stages. For the beginning cake baker they may be confusing. Here are the key terms and techniques.

WHIPPING. When ingredients such as egg whites or heavy cream are to be whipped into a froth, this usually indicates that the mixture includes those ingredients almost exclusively. Egg whites will not beat into a froth if there is even a speck of fat on the beater or in the bowl. Heavy cream, the bowl and beaters need to be chilled for proper whipping. Whip at high speed with a hand mixer, or in a large bowl with a wire whisk.

CREAMING. Creaming blends the butter and sugar together until the mixture is smooth and fluffy. Grandma did this in a bowl with a wooden spoon. We are most likely to use a hand mixer. Start at slow speed, scraping the bowl with a rubber spatula, then increase the speed until the mixture becomes light.

FOLDING. Folding involves scraping the edges of the bowl, pulling the rubber spatula up in the center of the bowl, turning the bowl, and continuing the motions until all ingredients are thoroughly blended.

BEATING. This process involves beating the ingredients together at a high speed — such as beating eggs and sugar together, or when adding eggs to a creamed mixture. Mixtures need to be beaten until thick and mousse-like. The beaters should easily leave a trail in the mixture when they are removed.

TIPS AND INSIGHTS

Baking beautiful cakes is undoubtedly an art, but there's a great deal of science and practical knowledge involved too. Lest this send you off into the cake mix aisle, let us say that "scratch" cakes offer variety and excitement to your repertoire — and a whole lot more flavor too. With tried and true recipes, such as those on the pages that follow, along with quality ingredients, the right baking pans, and a few practical tips, you can bake perfect cakes. Here are a few general rules.

- Start by reading the recipe from beginning to end.

- Use fresh ingredients.

- Preheat the oven in plenty of time.

- Have all ingredients at room temperature as, ingredients such as butter, sugar, eggs and flour will be easier to combine. Measure all the ingredients and do the basic preparation (such as grating a lemon or orange zest, peeling apples, chopping nuts) before you start.

- Use the appropriate measuring cup. For dry ingredients, use cups that measure level to the top of the cup. These cups are usually nested, ranging from ¼ cup to 1 cup in size. For liquid ingredients, use clear glass measuring cups and measure liquids with the cup on a level surface, and your eyes at cup level.

- Prepare the pans specified in the recipe before you start cooking. Pans that are of the wrong size will not give the proper results (too small and the batter overflows, too large and the cake will not have the volume desired).

- When beating egg whites, make sure that the bowl and beaters are scrupulously clean to ensure the greatest volume.

- Be sure to spread cake batter evenly into the pan.

- Once a cake batter is made, put it straight into the oven.

- To test when a cake is done, press the surface lightly with your fingertip. It should be springy to the touch. Another test is to insert a wooden toothpick into the center of the cake. It will come out clean if the cake is done. Also, many cakes will pull back slightly from the edges of the pan, indicating that the cake is baked.

- Use parchment paper for easy removal of the cake from the pan, especially when the recipe specifies it.

- Cool baked cakes on a rack before unmolding — or follow specific directions with the recipe.

- Always clean your pans carefully and dry them thoroughly to prevent grease buildup.

STRAWBERRY CREAM JELLY ROLL

A simple jelly roll needs to be included in every baker's repertoire. You can vary this one in many ways. When fresh raspberries are in season, roll them onto the cake instead of sliced strawberries. If strawberries are out of season, use just the jelly in the filling. This jelly roll is also pictured on pages 24-25.

3   eggs, at room temperature
1   cup sugar
1   teaspoon vanilla
1   cup all-purpose flour
2   teaspoons baking powder
½   teaspoon salt
⅓   cup powdered sugar plus 3 tablespoons
1   cup strawberry or raspberry jelly
1   cup whipping cream
1   pint sliced fresh strawberries
    Additional powdered sugar for top of roll

① Heat oven to 375°F. Grease 15x10x1-inch pan; line with parchment paper.

② In large bowl of electric mixer, beat eggs at highest speed until foamy, about 3 minutes. Add sugar, 1 tablespoon at a time, beating until very light and fluffy, about 5 minutes. Stir in vanilla.

③ In separate bowl, mix flour, baking powder and salt; fold into egg mixture until completely blended. Pour batter into pan; smooth out evenly. Bake 10 to 12 minutes or until top is dry when touched.

④ Meanwhile, sprinkle ⅓ cup powdered sugar over clean tea towel. Loosen sides of baked cake; invert onto towel. Remove parchment paper; roll cake up starting at a narrow end, rolling towel into cake. Place rolled cake on wire rack to cool.

⑤ Put jelly into microwave-safe bowl; warm slightly, stirring so that it is spreadable. Whip cream; gently fold in 3 tablespoons powdered sugar.

⑥ When cake is cooled, unroll; remove towel. Spread cake with jelly and whipped cream. Top evenly with strawberries. Re-roll; dust outside of roll with additional powdered sugar. Store in refrigerator.

ORANGE BUTTERMILK CAKE

Pour the hot orange syrup over the cake just as it comes out of the oven. The result is a juicy and moist dessert that could become your family's favorite.

CAKE
- 2 cups sugar
- 1 cup (2 sticks) butter, softened
- Grated peel of 2 oranges
- 2 eggs
- 1 cup diced dates
- 1 cup chopped walnuts
- 2½ cups all-purpose flour
- 1 teaspoon baking soda
- 1 teaspoon baking powder

SYRUP
- 1 cup buttermilk
- Juice of 2 oranges (about ¾ cup)

1. Heat oven to 350°F. Lightly grease 13x9-inch pan.

2. In mixing bowl, beat 1 cup of the sugar, butter and orange peel until light. Add eggs, one at a time, beating until light. Stir in dates and walnuts.

3. In separate bowl, mix flour, baking soda and baking powder; mix into butter mixture alternately with buttermilk until smooth. Pour into pan.

4. Bake 35 minutes or until toothpick inserted into center of cake comes out clean and dry. During last 5 minutes of baking, bring orange juice and remaining 1 cup sugar to a boil. Pierce hot, baked cake 8 to 10 times with fork; pour hot orange syrup over. Cool.

24 servings.

Preparation time: 20 minutes. Ready to serve: 1 hour, 55 minutes.

Per serving: 250 calories, 11.5 g total fat (5 g saturated fat), 40 mg cholesterol, 140 mg sodium, 1 g fiber.

APPLE DATE PECAN CAKE WITH CARAMEL SAUCE

A bit of cocoa and coffee in the batter heightens the flavor of the apples here. This moist, yet crunchy cake is delicious served with warm Caramel Sauce.

CAKE
1	cup sugar
1/2	cup (1 stick) butter, at room temperature
2	eggs
1 1/2	cups all-purpose flour
2	teaspoons unsweetened cocoa
1	teaspoon baking soda
1	teaspoon ground cinnamon
1/2	teaspoon ground cloves
2	cups peeled, chopped, tart cooking apples
1/2	cup chopped pitted dates
1	cup coarsely chopped pecans
1/2	cup cold coffee

CARAMEL SAUCE
1/4	cup (1/2 stick) butter
1/2	cup packed brown sugar
1/2	cup whipping cream
1	teaspoon vanilla

1. Heat oven to 350°F. Lightly grease 10-inch springform pan or 13x9-inch pan.

2. In mixing bowl, beat sugar and 1/2 cup butter at medium speed until light and fluffy; beat in eggs until light. Combine flour, cocoa, baking soda, cinnamon and cloves.

3. In small bowl, combine apples, dates and pecans. Mix 2 tablespoons of flour mixture into apples until all pieces are coated with flour. Mix remaining flour into butter mixture alternately with coffee until batter is smooth. Stir in apple mixture until well blended. Pour batter into pan; bake 35 to 40 minutes or until cake bounces back when touched in center. Cut cake into wedges while still warm; serve with warm Caramel Sauce.

4. To make Caramel Sauce: In small saucepan, melt 1/4 cup butter. Stir in brown sugar over low heat 2 minutes until sugar is dissolved. Add cream; heat just to a boil. Remove from heat; stir in vanilla. Serve warm.

12 servings.

Preparation time: 40 minutes. Ready to serve: 2 hours, 10 minutes.

Per serving: 580 calories, 23 g total fat (10 g saturated fat), 80 mg cholesterol, 200 mg sodium, 7.5 g fiber.

CAPPUCCINO SPONGE CAKE

This basic sponge cake is one of the easiest you'll ever make.

CAKE
- 1⅓ cups eggs (about 6 large), at room temperature
- 1⅓ cups each sugar, all-purpose flour
- ⅛ teaspoon salt
- 2 tablespoons instant-coffee granules
- 1 tablespoon water

FILLING AND FROSTING
- ¼ cup plus 1 tablespoon milk
- 2 tablespoons instant-coffee granules
- 1 cup semisweet chocolate morsels, melted
- 6 cups whipping cream
- ⅓ cup powdered sugar

GARNISH
- Chocolate covered coffee beans (optional)

❶ Heat oven to 350°F. Butter two 9-inch round cake pans; line with parchment paper. Dust with flour.

❷ In large bowl of electric mixer, beat eggs until frothy. Add sugar, 1 to 2 tablespoons at a time, beating at high speed until very light and lemon colored. Beat 5 minutes after all the sugar has been added. In separate bowl, mix flour and salt. Reduce speed to low; add flour mixture. Mix 30 seconds. Dissolve 2 tablespoons instant coffee in water. With rubber spatula, fold coffee into batter, scraping sides of bowl. Divide batter between pans. Bake 20 to 25 minutes or until cakes pull away from sides of pans and center of cake springs back when lightly touched. Remove from oven; cool on wire rack in pan 10 minutes. Remove from pan; cool on rack until completely cooled. Split layers horizontally into 2 layers each.

❸ Meanwhile, prepare filling and frosting. Pour ¼ cup of the milk and 1 tablespoon of the instant coffee into small bowl, stirring until coffee is dissolved. Slowly stir into melted chocolate until smooth. Cool completely.

❹ Whip 1 cup of the cream; gently fold into chocolate mixture. In small bowl, mix remaining 1 tablespoon milk and 1 tablespoon coffee. Whip remaining 5 cups cream until stiff; slowly whip in coffee mixture and powdered sugar.

❺ Cover 1 cake layer half with ⅓ of chocolate mixture. Top with second half of cake layer; spread with ⅓ of chocolate mixture. Top with half of remaining cake layer; spread with remaining chocolate mixture. Top with second half of second layer. Frost top and sides of cake with coffee flavored whipped cream. Garnish with chocolate covered coffee beans, if desired. Refrigerate until ready to serve. Store in refrigerator.

16 servings.

Preparation time: 45 minutes. Ready to serve: 3 hours, 45 minutes.

Per serving: 460 calories, 33 g total fat (20 g saturated fat), 185 mg cholesterol, 80 mg sodium, 1 g fiber.

GINGERED CARROT SPICE CAKE

Little bits of candied ginger create a pleasant surprise in this twist on the traditional carrot cake. It's made with a simple one-bowl mixing method.

CAKE

2	cups all-purpose flour
2	cups sugar
1	teaspoon baking powder
1	teaspoon baking soda
1	teaspoon ground cinnamon
2	tablespoons finely chopped crystallized ginger
3	cups finely shredded carrots
1	cup vegetable oil
4	eggs

CREAM CHEESE FROSTING

2	(3-oz.) pkg. cream cheese
1/2	cup (1 stick) butter
2	teaspoons vanilla
3 1/4 to 3 1/2	cups powdered sugar

1. Heat oven to 350°F. Grease and flour two 9-inch round cake pans or one 13x9-inch pan.

2. In large bowl of electric mixer, combine flour, sugar, baking powder, baking soda, cinnamon and ginger. Add carrots, oil and eggs. Beat at low speed 1 minute, scraping bowl once or twice. Beat at high speed 2 to 3 minutes until batter is light. Pour into pan.

3. Bake 30 to 35 minutes for round pans or 35 to 40 minutes for 13x9-inch pan or until toothpick inserted in center of cake comes out clean. Cool. Spread with frosting.

4. To make Cream Cheese Frosting: In medium bowl, beat cream cheese, butter and vanilla until light and fluffy. Add 2 cups of the powdered sugar, beating well. Gradually beat in remaining powdered sugar to reach spreading consistency.

12 servings.

Preparation time: 40 minutes. Ready to serve: 2 hours, 20 minutes.

Per serving: 655 calories, 33 g total fat (11 g saturated fat), 105 mg cholesterol, 275 mg sodium, 1.5 g fiber.

SPICED PUMPKIN CREAM CHEESE POUND CAKE

Pumpkin and cream cheese keep this cake incredibly moist. This is a large recipe, so be sure you measure your baking pan's capacity. Or, if you choose, divide the batter between two 9x5-inch loaf pans.

3	cups all-purpose flour
2	cups sugar
2	tablespoons pumpkin pie spice
1½	teaspoons baking powder
1½	teaspoons baking soda
½	teaspoon salt
1	cup (2 sticks) butter, softened
1	(8-oz.) pkg. cream cheese, softened
3	eggs
1	(15-oz.) can pumpkin puree
1	teaspoon vanilla

① Heat oven to 350°F. Grease and flour 12-cup* fancy tube-style cake pan; dust with sugar. Or grease and flour two 9x5-inch loaf pans.

② In large bowl of electric mixer, combine flour, sugar, pumpkin pie spice, baking powder, baking soda and salt.

③ Cut butter and cream cheese into chunks; blend into dry ingredients. Beat in eggs, pumpkin and vanilla at medium speed until batter is light and fluffy. Pour batter into pan; smooth top evenly.

④ Bake 1 hour to 1 hour 10 minutes or until wooden skewer inserted into center of cake comes out clean and dry. Cool cake in pan on wire rack 20 minutes. Turn out onto rack; cool completely.

12 servings.

Preparation time: 15 minutes. Ready to serve: 1 hour, 35 minutes.

Per serving: 480 calories, 24 g total fat (14 g saturated fat), 115 mg cholesterol, 490 mg sodium, 2 g fiber.

TIP *If in doubt about pan size, measure water into the cake pan. If your pan measures less than 12 cups (usually it will be a 10-cup pan), spoon about 2 cups batter into 6 greased cupcake or custard cups. Bake along with 10-inch cake 20 to 25 minutes or until cakes test done.

SWEDISH FILBERT CAKE WITH WHITE CHOCOLATE BUTTERCREAM FROSTING AND FILLING

Loaded with filberts, this cake slices beautifully, and the flavor actually becomes nuttier within a day or two after baking. Keep the cake refrigerated up to one week, or freeze it up to two months for make-ahead convenience.

CAKE
- 4 eggs
- 1⅓ cups sugar
- 2 cups filberts, toasted, skinned, pulverized
- 1⅓ cups all-purpose flour
- 2 teaspoons baking powder
- ½ cup (1 stick) butter, melted
- 1 cup milk

WHITE CHOCOLATE BUTTERCREAM
- 2 (3-oz.) bars white chocolate
- 1 (8-oz.) pkg. cream cheese, softened
- ½ cup (1 stick) unsalted butter, softened
- 1 tablespoon lemon juice

1. Heat oven to 350°F. Butter two 9-inch round cake pans; dust with flour. Shake out excess flour.

2. In large bowl of electric mixer, beat eggs and sugar at medium speed until light and fluffy. Fold filberts into egg mixture. Stir flour and baking powder together; sift through strainer into mixture. Fold into egg mixture along with melted butter and milk.

3. Divide batter between pans; smooth tops evenly. Bake 25 to 30 minutes or until toothpick inserted into center of cake comes out clean. Cool in pan on wire rack 10 minutes. Loosen edges of layers; turn cakes out onto racks to cool completely.

4. To make White Chocolate Buttercream: Break white chocolate up; place in bowl. Set over very hot water; stir until chocolate begins to melt. Remove from heat. Beat cream cheese until smooth and creamy; blend in white chocolate, softened butter and lemon juice. Beat until very smooth.

5. Place first cake layer top-side down on serving plate. Cover with ½ cup buttercream. Top with second layer, top-side up. Spread top and sides with remaining buttercream. Chill cake until buttercream is firm, 2 to 3 hours.

16 servings.

Preparation time: 45 minutes. Ready to serve: 3 hours, 50 minutes.

Per serving: 445 calories, 32 g total fat (13.5 g saturated fat), 105 mg cholesterol, 175 mg sodium, 1 g fiber.

BANANA BLITZ TORTE

In German "Blitz" means lightning — this old-fashioned yellow cake is quick to mix! The egg yolks go into the cake, and the whites are whipped into a meringue that bakes directly on top of each layer. Layered with sliced bananas and cream, it's spectacular and delicious!

1	cup all-purpose flour
1	teaspoon baking powder
1/4	teaspoon salt
1 1/4	cups sugar
1/2	cup (1 stick) butter, softened
1/3	cup milk
3	eggs, separated
1	teaspoon vanilla
1/4	cup sliced almonds
1/2	cup whipping cream
2	tablespoons powdered sugar
2	bananas, peeled, sliced

❶ Heat oven to 350°F. Butter two 8- or 9-inch round cake pans; dust lightly with flour.

❷ In large bowl, combine flour, baking powder, salt and 1/2 cup of the sugar; mix in butter until completely blended. In separate bowl, mix milk with egg yolks and vanilla; add to dry ingredients. Beat until light and fluffy. Divide batter between cake pans.

❸ In clean bowl with clean, dry beaters, beat egg whites until soft peaks form; add remaining 3/4 cup sugar, 1 tablespoon at a time, beating well after each addition until egg whites stand in stiff peaks when beaters are lifted.

❹ Divide meringue evenly between pans, smoothing with spatula over tops. Sprinkle almonds over meringue layers. Bake 20 to 25 minutes or until meringue is golden and a toothpick inserted in center of layers comes out clean. Cool in pans 10 minutes. With small spatula or knife, loosen layers from sides of the pans. Invert onto wire racks, then invert again so meringues are on top. Cool completely, about 1 hour.

❺ In small bowl, whip cream until stiff; add powdered sugar. Place 1 cake layer with meringue-side up on cake plate; top with bananas and whipped cream. Place second layer, meringue-side up, on top of bananas and cream. Store in refrigerator.

16 servings.

Preparation time: 40 minutes. Ready to serve: 2 hours, 5 minutes.

Per serving: 205 calories, 10 g total fat (5.5 g saturated fat), 65 mg cholesterol, 120 mg sodium, 1 g fiber.

TOSCA CAKE

Tosca Cake is Scandinavian in origin, where they like to name their favorite cakes in "operatic" style. Here, the "stage" is one of the finest yellow cakes you've ever tasted, topped with glistening caramel and almonds. The best part? This creation is really easy to make.

CAKE
- 1 cup whipping cream
- 2 eggs
- 1 teaspoon vanilla
- 1½ cups all-purpose flour
- 1 cup sugar
- 2 teaspoons baking powder
- ½ teaspoon salt

CARAMEL TOPPING
- ⅓ cup butter
- ⅓ cup sugar
- ¾ cup sliced almonds
- 1 tablespoon all-purpose flour
- 1 tablespoon whipping cream

1. Heat oven to 350°F. Butter 10-inch springform pan or 13x9-inch pan.

2. In large bowl of electric mixer, beat 1 cup cream until stiff; beat in eggs and vanilla. In small bowl, stir together 1½ cups flour, 1 cup sugar, baking powder and salt. Beat flour mixture into cream mixture until smooth. Pour into pan.

3. Bake 30 to 35 minutes or until cake pulls away from sides of pan and toothpick inserted into center of cake comes out clean and dry.

4. Meanwhile, make Caramel Topping: In small saucepan, melt butter over medium heat. Add ⅓ cup sugar, almonds, 1 tablespoon flour and 1 tablespoon cream. Stirring constantly, bring to a boil. Cook, stirring occasionally, about 3 to 5 minutes or until slightly thickened.

5. Pour hot topping over hot cake, completely covering top. Bake 10 to 15 minutes longer or until golden brown. Serve warm or cold.

12 servings.

Preparation time: 15 minutes. Ready to serve: 1 hour, 54 minutes.

Per serving: 300 calories, 15.5 g total fat (8 g saturated fat), 70 mg cholesterol, 230 mg sodium, 1 g fiber.

FLOURLESS CHOCOLATE GRAND MARNIER CAKE

There is no flour in this cake, but its texture is light and the chocolate flavor predominates. In addition, it's another easy one to make!

12 oz. bittersweet or semisweet chocolate, cut into pieces
3/4 cup (1 1/2 sticks) unsalted butter, cut into pieces
6 eggs, separated
3/4 cup sugar
3 tablespoons Grand Marnier
1 teaspoon powdered sugar

1 Heat oven to 350°F. Line 10-inch springform pan with parchment paper. Coat with nonstick cooking spray.

2 In heavy saucepan, melt chocolate and butter over low heat, stirring occasionally; remove from heat. Cool to room temperature.

3 Place egg yolks in large mixing bowl; place egg whites in another. Beat egg yolks with electric mixer at high speed, adding 6 tablespoons of the sugar until mixture is thick and pale, about 3 minutes. Fold in chocolate mixture and Grand Marnier.

4 Wash beaters. Beat egg whites until soft peaks form. Gradually add remaining 6 tablespoons sugar, beating until firm peaks form. Fold 1/3 of egg whites at a time into chocolate mixture. Pour batter into pan.

5 Bake 50 minutes or until toothpick inserted into center comes out with some moist crumbs attached. Cool in pan on wire rack. Gently press down crusty top to make evenly thick cake.

6 Using small knife, loosen edges. Remove pan sides. Invert onto flat pan. Remove parchment from bottom. Carefully invert onto serving plate. Dust with powdered sugar to garnish.

16 servings.

Preparation time: 30 minutes. Ready to serve: 3 hours, 10 minutes.

Per serving: 250 calories, 20 g total fat (11 g saturated fat), 100 mg cholesterol, 30 mg sodium, 2 g fiber.

CHEESECAKES

by Charla Draper

While it's true that a cheescake isn't the easiest dessert you'll ever create, it's also a fact that a good cheesecake might be one of the most magnificent and raved-over culinary delights you ever produce. Here's how to do cheesecake right — and with a minimum of fuss.

Pumpkin Swirl Cheesecake, page 48

ESSENTIALS — CHEESECAKES

History shows that cheesecake appeared in Europe as early as 1440; but this 15th century version was distinctly different from the cheesecakes we are fond of today.

With European immigration and the influence of German bakers on the food scene in 18th century Philadelphia, the popularity of the dessert grew. One of the earliest recorded recipes for the dessert appeared in an imported cookbook readily available in the Pennsylvania-German community. During the 1850s the book was finally published in Philadelphia as The Complete Cookbook for the German-American Kitchen. *It included the recipe* Cheesecake the Common Way, *which had long been a favorite in local German households.*

In efforts to re-create the Neufchâtel cheese of France, a key ingredient in early cheesecake recipes, American dairymen invented a new product in 1872. Their unripened cheese invention was richer and creamier than Neufchâtel. With these textural properties, cream cheese seemed to be the most logical moniker for the new food. Cheesecake was on its way.

INGREDIENTS

The key to creating good cheesecake is to start with ingredients that are the foundation for many extraordinarily good desserts. Cheesecakes contain eggs, sugar and of course cheese; this trio combines to form the basics of cheesecake. And it is the cheese that contributes most significantly to the character and texture of the finished dessert.

CHEESE. Cheesecakes are traditionally made from fresh cheeses — cream cheese, mascarpone, Neufchâtel, ricotta, cottage cheese and farmer cheese. These fresh or unripened cheese products are characterized by their butterfat content. Though each of these unripened cheeses contains approximately the same amount of cheese solids (15% to 18%), it is their fat that defines them. As the fat content increases, the smoother, creamier and richer the cheese ... and the cheesecake it creates.

Cream cheese is an American innovation. It has a smooth, creamy texture, is made from cow's milk, and must contain at least 33% milk fat and no more than 55% moisture.

Mascarpone is an Italian cream cheese. It is made from cow's milk and the flavor is rich and buttery. It blends easily with other flavors and is sometimes sold with fruit in it.

Neufchâtel Cheese is from the French town of Neufchâtel. It is made from cow's milk with milk fat between 20% to 45%. American Neufchâtel is made from whole or skim milk or is a combination of milk and cream. This cheese is soft and white, with a mild, slightly salty flavor. The butterfat content is about 23% and the moisture content is 60%.

Ricotta Cheese is made in the United States. It is a combination of whey and whole or skim milk. The fat content is usually 4% to 10% with about 72% moisture. This cheese is slightly grainy in texture and has a slightly sweet flavor.

Cottage Cheese can be made with skim milk, whole milk or have cream added. Butterfat content will range from ½% to 4%. Cottage cheese is moist and can be purchased with different size curds ranging from small to large. It is available as creamed cottage cheese (4% to 8% fat); low fat (1% to 2%) fat or nonfat.

Farmer Cheese is a type of cottage cheese with most of its liquid removed. It has a mild and slightly tangy flavor, and can be sliced or crumbled.

EGGS. Eggs contribute different characteristics to baked goods. When added whole, the eggs can leaven, lighten and contribute structure-holding dishes together. Egg yolks hold the structure together and they emulsify, holding fat and moisture to produce a smooth and creamy texture. Egg whites leaven and hold the structure together. Whites also function as a drying agent that absorbs moisture. In cheesecakes, eggs can be used to accomplish any or all of these features.

SUGAR. Sugar in baked goods tenderizes and adds moisture. In cheesecakes, sugar works primarily to sweeten the dessert. In recipes with flour, sugar tenderizes, interfering with the development of gluten, that element of flour that forms the structure of baked foods and can make them tough.

BEYOND THE BASIC TRIO. Along with the basic three ingredients described (cheese, eggs and sugar), cheesecakes can include flour, cream, gelatin, flavorings, fruit or nuts — each influencing the consistency of the finished dessert. Though each of these ingredients are not likely to be found in the same cake, with an appropriate pairing from the list they will create a cheesecake that adds a memorable final flourish to any menu.

TOOLS

There are only two tools I recommend having on hand at a moment's notice when you want to create the perfect cheesecake.

SPRINGFORM PAN. The first piece of equipment you should have on hand is the **springform pan**. This pan is readily available in most cookware stores. Its use has grown in popularity along with consumer interest in cheesecake. Springform pans range in diameter from 8 to 12 inches. Some stores even carry miniature 4-inch pans for individual cheesecakes. Larger sizes may also be available from equipment vendors for commercial food service operations. The pan's convenience factor is that the spring-lock mechanism on the outside rim allows the pan sides to be removed. The completed cheesecake is then intact for garnishing and serving.

ELECTRIC MIXER. The second piece of equipment needed for making cheesecakes is an **electric mixer** to help you thoroughly blend the ingredients.

TERMS AND TECHNIQUES

To successfully make cheesecakes, as with other recipes, it is important to get the right start — by reading the recipe first. The basic preparation of cheesecakes is straightforward. Yet an understanding of the following terms and techniques will help you achieve cheesecake perfection.

WHIPPED CREAM. Use cream that is labeled "heavy cream" or "whipping cream" on the carton; this cream contains 30% to 40% fat. Whip the cream to the stiff stage. Whipped cream will increase two to three times in volume. When whipped to stiff, the whipped cream should fall in soft blobs, forming soft peaks when the beater is removed, and still look glossy. For best results, chill the cream first, then whip the cream with chilled beaters in a chilled, large and deep bowl.

BEAT EGGS IN A BOWL THAT IS NOT ALUMINUM OR PLASTIC. Aluminum will cause the eggs to gray, and plastic can retain fat in the bowl, which will inhibit successful beating of the egg whites. Eggs are easier to separate when cold. However, they will create a better foam when they are at room temperature.

EGG WHITES FORM SOFT PEAKS. Whip/beat the egg whites until frothy, incorporating air until they increase in volume and form peaks that remain when the beaters are removed. The tip of the peak will remain upright and won't tip over.

46

SEPARATED EGGS. Separate the egg yolks from the egg whites by firmly cracking the egg on the edge of one bowl, creating 2 halves of eggshell. While holding the eggshell over the bowl, pour the egg back and forth, allowing the egg white to flow into the bowl. Do not allow any yolk to mix with the egg white. The presence of any fat or egg yolk will interfere with successfully beating and whipping the egg white. Place the remaining yolk in a second bowl. Pour the egg white into the clean mixing bowl. Repeat with remaining whole eggs.

SCALDED MILK. Heat milk, half-and-half or cream to just below the boiling point. Tiny bubbles will form around the edge of the pan. The milk should not boil when scalded.

TIPS AND INSIGHTS

Cheesecakes may crack on the surface; this can be caused by temperature variations between the cake center and the edge of the pan while the cake bakes. Other suggestions to guard against the "cracking phenomena" are to:

- Bake the cheesecakes at temperatures between 300°F and 350°F.

- If all else fails and the cheese-cake develops a crack or two, flavored sour cream, fruit or topping can camouflage the break with panache, keeping this little secret under cover!

- Do not overcook; cheesecakes are done when the center just barely jiggles. According to Shirley Corriher, author and authority on cooking fixes, "Cheesecakes crack as a result of overcooking. When completely cooked, a 3-inch circle in the cake center is still wobbly and shaky."

- Equalize heat throughout the cake by baking in a hot water bath. To do this, place the cheesecake pan *inside* a second pan that is large and deep enough so that water will be 1½ inches deep, surrounding the cheesecake pan. It is a good idea to place a thick towel under the cheesecake pan (between the two pans) to protect the cheesecake from heat on the bottom. Place the pans on the oven's middle shelf. Carefully pour nearly boiling water into the second pan, then slide the shelf back into the oven. Cook the cheesecake as directed; remove the cheesecake from the hot water bath when it is done.

PUMPKIN SWIRL CHEESECAKE

There is a cheesecake for every season. Pumpkin Swirl Cheesecake *(pictured on pages 42-43) will certainly be dessert-of-the-day during autumn celebrations.*

CRUST
- 1½ cups graham cracker crumbs
- 3 tablespoons sugar
- 6 tablespoons butter or margarine, melted

FILLING
- 3 (8-oz.) pkg. cream cheese, softened
- ¾ cup sugar
- 3 tablespoons all-purpose flour
- 3 eggs
- ½ cup sour cream
- 1½ teaspoons vanilla
- ¼ cup packed brown sugar
- ¾ teaspoon ground cinnamon
- ½ teaspoon each ground nutmeg, ginger, allspice
- 1½ cups pumpkin puree
- 2 tablespoons maple syrup

TOPPING
- 1 cup sour cream
- 2 tablespoons packed brown sugar

GARNISH
- ⅓ cup pecan halves, sugared if desired

1. Heat oven to 325°F. In medium bowl, combine graham cracker crumbs, 3 tablespoons sugar and butter; mix until blended. Press crumb mixture into bottom and up sides of 9-inch springform pan. Bake 10 minutes. Remove from oven; cool.

2. In mixing bowl, combine cream cheese, ¾ cup sugar and 2 tablespoons of the flour; beat at medium speed until well blended. Add eggs, one at a time, mixing well after each addition. Blend in ½ cup sour cream and vanilla. Remove approximately 3 cups batter; set aside.

3. In medium bowl, combine ¼ cup brown sugar, remaining 1 tablespoon flour, cinnamon, nutmeg, ginger and allspice; mix to blend. Mix pumpkin, brown sugar mixture and maple syrup into remaining batter; stir until blended. Spoon ½ of pumpkin mixture into crust. Gently spoon ½ of plain batter over pumpkin batter. Continue alternating layers of batter until pan is full. With metal spatula or knife, gently swirl spatula through batters for marbled effect. Bake 1 hour 5 minutes or until center is set. Remove from oven; loosen cake from rim of pan. Cool completely before removing rim of pan. Chill several hours or overnight.

4. In small bowl, combine 1 cup sour cream and 2 tablespoons brown sugar. Spread on top of cooled cheesecake. Top with pecans. Store in refrigerator.

12 servings.

Preparation time: 40 minutes. Ready to serve: 3 hours, 25 minutes.

Per serving: 500 calories, 35.5 g total fat (20.5 g saturated fat), 150 mg cholesterol, 300 mg sodium, 1.5 g fiber.

TIRAMISU CHEESECAKE

Flavored with mascarpone cheese and coffee liqueur, this cheesecake is sure to be another ethereal dessert.

CRUST
- 1½ cups graham cracker crumbs
- ¼ cup (½ stick) butter or margarine, melted
- 1 teaspoon coffee-flavored liqueur

FILLING
- 1 (8-oz.) pkg. cream cheese, softened
- 8 oz. mascarpone cheese
- ½ cup sugar
- 3 eggs, separated
- ¼ cup coffee-flavored liqueur
- 1 teaspoon vanilla
- ⅛ teaspoon cream of tartar

1. Heat oven to 350°F.

2. In medium bowl, combine graham cracker crumbs, butter and 1 teaspoon liqueur; mix until well blended. Press crumb mixture into bottom and up sides of 9-inch springform pan. Bake 8 to 10 minutes. Remove from oven; cool.

3. In mixing bowl, combine cream cheese, mascarpone and sugar; beat at medium speed until blended. Add egg yolks; mix well after each addition. Blend in ¼ cup liqueur and vanilla; set aside.

4. In clean mixing bowl, combine egg whites and cream of tartar; beat at high speed until soft peaks form. Fold into cheese mixture. Pour into crust; bake 50 to 60 minutes or until center is almost set.

5. Remove from oven; loosen cake from sides of pan. Cool completely before removing rim of pan. Chill several hours or overnight. Store in refrigerator.

12 servings.

Preparation time: 35 minutes. Ready to serve: 3 hours, 55 minutes.

Per serving: 275 calories, 19 g total fat (11 g saturated fat), 105 mg cholesterol, 210 mg sodium, 0 g fiber.

APPLE CREAM CHEESE BARS

Enjoy these cheesecake-y bars on-the-go, in brown bag lunches or as a late day snack. Although not as formal as traditional cheesecake, they're definitely as tasty!

CRUST
1½ cups all-purpose flour
½ cup packed light brown sugar
¼ cup (½ stick) butter or margarine
1 egg
1 teaspoon vanilla

FILLING
1 (8-oz.) pkg. cream cheese
¼ cup plus ⅓ cup sugar
1 egg
½ teaspoon vanilla
2½ cups thinly sliced peeled baking apples
1 tablespoon lemon juice
1 teaspoon ground cinnamon
1 teaspoon ground nutmeg
Caramel or butterscotch ice cream topping (optional)

1. Heat oven to 400°F. In mixing bowl, combine flour, brown sugar, butter, egg and 1 teaspoon vanilla; beat at medium speed until crumbly. Press crumb mixture into bottom and up sides of 8- or 9-inch square pan. Bake 6 to 8 minutes or until lightly browned. Remove from oven; cool.

2. Increase oven temperature to 450°F. In another medium bowl, combine cream cheese and ¼ cup of the sugar; mix well. Mix in egg and ½ teaspoon vanilla until well blended.

3. In separate bowl, toss apples with lemon juice. Add remaining ⅓ cup sugar, cinnamon and nutmeg; mix lightly. Pour cream cheese mixture into crust; spoon apple mixture over cream cheese. Bake 10 minutes. Reduce oven temperature to 400°F; bake an additional 25 minutes or until knife inserted in center comes out clean. Cool. Cut into squares. Serve with warm ice cream topping, if desired. Store in refrigerator.

9 servings.

Preparation time: 35 minutes. Ready to serve: 2 hours, 15 minutes.

Per serving: 345 calories, 15.5 g total fat (9 g saturated fat), 90 mg cholesterol, 130 mg sodium, 1.5 g fiber.

AMARETTO CHIFFON CHEESECAKE

This is a quick and elegant dessert for a busy schedule with cheesecake on the menu. Once your guests taste this masterpiece, they'll never know how easy it was to make.

CRUST
1½   cups finely crushed vanilla wafers
1   tablespoon sugar
¼   cup (½ stick) butter or margarine, melted
1   teaspoon almond-flavored liqueur

FILLING
2   (8-oz.) pkg. cream cheese, softened
½   cup half-and-half or milk
1   teaspoon vanilla
1   (3.4-oz.) pkg. instant vanilla pudding and pie filling
½   cup almond-flavored liqueur

GARNISH
Toasted slivered almonds (optional)

① Heat oven to 350°F.

② In medium bowl, combine crushed vanilla wafers and sugar; blend in butter and 1 teaspoon liqueur; mix well. Reserve 2 tablespoons crumb mixture; set aside. Press remaining crumb mixture into bottom and up sides of 9-inch springform pan or 9-inch pie plate. Bake 10 minutes. Remove from oven; cool.

③ In large bowl, combine cream cheese and ¼ cup of the half-and-half; beat at medium speed until smooth. Add vanilla; beat at high speed 1 minute. Reduce speed to medium. Gradually add instant pudding; blend in remaining ½ cup half-and-half, mixing well. Add ½ cup liqueur. Beat at high speed until mixture is well blended and slightly fluffy.

④ Pour cream cheese mixture into crust; sprinkle with reserved crumbs. Cover; chill 2 to 3 hours or overnight. Garnish with almonds, if desired. Store in refrigerator.

10 servings.

Preparation time: 30 minutes. Ready to serve: 3 hours, 40 minutes.

Per serving: 355 calories, 25 g total fat (15 g saturated fat), 70 mg cholesterol, 365 mg sodium, 0 g fiber.

NEW YORK STYLE CHEESECAKE WITH RED, WHITE & BLUEBERRIES

Created in the style of the cheesecake made famous at Lindy's *restaurant in New York City, America's most popular fruits are the only topping to consider with this classic dessert.*

CRUST
1½ cups finely crushed vanilla wafers
1 tablespoon sugar
½ teaspoon vanilla powder
5 tablespoons butter or margarine, melted

FILLING
2 (8-oz.) pkg. cream cheese, softened
1 cup sugar
1 (8-oz.) pkg. light ricotta cheese
4 eggs
⅓ cup sour cream
1 teaspoon vanilla

1 tablespoon lemon juice
2 teaspoons grated lemon peel

TOPPING
1 (15-oz.) can cherry pie filling
½ cup sour cream
2 teaspoons powdered sugar
¼ teaspoon grated lemon peel
1 cup sliced strawberries
2 tablespoons kirsch
½ cup blueberries

GARNISH
Mint leaves (optional)

1. Heat oven to 325°F. In medium bowl, combine crushed vanilla wafers, 1 tablespoon sugar, vanilla powder and butter; mix until blended. Press crumb mixture into bottom and up sides of 9-inch springform pan. Bake 10 minutes. Remove from oven; cool.

2. In medium bowl, combine cream cheese and 1 cup sugar; beat at medium speed until well blended. Blend in ricotta. Add eggs, one at a time, mixing well after each addition. Blend in ⅓ cup sour cream, vanilla, lemon juice and 2 teaspoons lemon peel. Pour into crust. Bake 1 hour 5 minutes or until center is almost set. Remove from oven; loosen cake from sides of pan. Cool completely before removing rim of pan. Chill several hours or overnight. Using strainer or colander, strain cherries from syrup, reserving syrup. In medium bowl, mix together ½ cup sour cream, powdered sugar and ¼ teaspoon lemon peel. Spread over top of cheesecake.

3. In separate bowl, combine cherries, strawberries and kirsch; toss lightly. Pour strawberry mixture into reserved syrup; mix lightly. Spoon mixture over sour cream; top with blueberries. Garnish with mint leaves, if desired. Store in refrigerator.

12 servings.

Preparation time: 50 minutes. Ready to serve: 3 hours, 55 minutes.

Per serving: 430 calories, 26.5 g total fat (15.5 g saturated fat), 140 mg cholesterol, 240 mg sodium, 1.5 g fiber.

AMBROSIA CHEESECAKE SQUARES

Created to duplicate the flavor and ingredients of the well-known fruit filled dish, this recipe demonstrates cheesecake's versatility.

CRUST

- 6 tablespoons butter, at room temperature
- 1/3 cup packed brown sugar
- 3/4 cup all-purpose flour
- 1/4 cup graham cracker crumbs
- 2 tablespoons finely chopped almonds

FILLING

- 1 (8-oz.) pkg. cream cheese, softened
- 1/2 cup sugar
- 1 tablespoon all-purpose flour
- 1 egg
- 1/4 cup milk
- 1/2 teaspoon orange extract
- 1/4 teaspoon almond extract
- 1 (8-oz.) can crushed pineapple in juice, drained, juice reserved

TOPPING

- Orange juice
- 2 tablespoons cornstarch
- 1 (8-oz.) can mandarin orange segments, drained
- 1 (8-oz.) can pineapple chunks or tidbits, drained

GARNISH

- Maraschino cherries (optional)
- Shredded toasted coconut (optional)

1. Heat oven to 375°F. Lightly grease and flour 9-inch square pan. In large bowl, combine butter, brown sugar, 3/4 cup flour, graham cracker crumbs and almonds; beat at medium speed until well mixed. Press crumb mixture into bottom and slightly up sides of pan. Bake 8 to 10 minutes or until lightly browned. Reduce oven temperature to 350°F.

2. In large bowl, combine cream cheese, sugar and 1 tablespoon flour with electric mixer at medium speed until smooth. Add egg; mix well. Blend in milk, orange extract and almond extract; stir in pineapple, mixing well. Pour cream cheese mixture into crust. Bake 20 to 25 minutes or until knife inserted in center comes out clean. Cool completely.

3. Combine reserved pineapple juice and enough orange juice to measure 3/4 cup. In small saucepan, gradually add juice mixture to cornstarch; mix until smooth. Whisk over medium heat until thickened. Arrange orange segments and pineapple on top of cheesecake; spoon glaze over fruit. Chill 2 to 3 hours or overnight. To serve, cut into squares. Garnish with cherries and coconut, if desired. Store in refrigerator.

12 servings.

Preparation time: 2 hours. Ready to serve: 3 hours, 5 minutes.

Per serving: 265 calories, 14 g total fat (8 g saturated fat), 55 mg cholesterol, 115 mg sodium, 1 g fiber.

MANGO CHEESECAKE

Fresh mangoes, mango sorbet and tropical fruit add exotic flavor to this refreshing cheesecake. In mid-winter, this cheesecake may be just the thing to combat the cold weather blues.

CRUST
- 1 cup graham cracker crumbs
- ½ cup finely crushed gingersnap cookies
- ¼ cup (½ stick) butter or margarine, melted
- 1 tablespoon sugar

FILLING
- 2 (8-oz.) pkg. cream cheese, softened
- ⅓ cup sugar
- 2 tablespoons all-purpose flour
- 3 eggs
- 1½ cups mango puree
- ¾ cup mango sorbet, softened

TOPPING
- 2 tablespoons cornstarch
- 1 tablespoon sugar
- 1 cup mango nectar
- ⅓ cup mango puree
- 2 tablespoons coconut rum
- Mango chunks
- Sliced kiwi fruit
- Sliced star fruit

1. Heat oven to 350°F. In medium bowl, combine graham cracker crumbs, crushed gingersnaps, butter and 1 tablespoon sugar; mix until blended. Press crumb mixture into bottom and slightly up sides of 9-inch springform pan. Bake 8 to 10 minutes. Remove from oven; cool.

2. In large bowl, combine cream cheese, ⅓ cup sugar and flour; beat at medium speed until blended. Add eggs, one at a time, mixing well after each addition. Blend in 1½ cups mango puree and mango sorbet. Pour mixture into crust; bake 50 to 60 minutes or until center is set. Remove from oven; loosen from sides of pan. Cool completely before removing rim of pan. Chill several hours or overnight.

3. In saucepan, combine cornstarch and 1 tablespoon sugar. Stir in mango nectar and ⅓ cup mango puree. Heat over medium heat, stirring constantly, 1 to 2 minutes or until thickened. Stir in rum. Remove from heat. Arrange mango chunks, kiwi fruit and star fruit on top of cheesecake; spoon mango glaze over fruit. Store in refrigerator.

12 servings.

Preparation time: 50 minutes. Ready to serve: 4 hours.

Per serving: 325 calories, 19.5 g total fat (11.5 g saturated fat), 105 mg cholesterol, 215 mg sodium, 1.5 g fiber.

CHOCOLATE DECADENCE CHEESECAKE

Created for the chocoholic, this recipe is unequivocally chocolate from top to bottom.

CRUST
- 1½ cups creme-filled chocolate sandwich cookie crumbs
- ¼ cup sugar
- ½ teaspoon ground cinnamon
- ¼ cup (½ stick) butter or margarine, melted

FILLING
- ¾ cup whipping cream
- 4 oz. bittersweet chocolate, melted
- 2 (8-oz.) pkg. cream cheese, softened
- 1 cup sugar
- 2 tablespoons Dutch-process cocoa
- ½ teaspoon ground cinnamon
- 3 eggs, separated
- 1 teaspoon vanilla
- ⅛ teaspoon cream of tartar

TOPPING
- ¼ cup whipping cream
- 2 oz. bittersweet chocolate, melted
- 1 teaspoon vanilla
- 1 cup whipped cream

GARNISH
- Chocolate curls (optional)
- Toasted slivered almonds (optional)
- Fresh strawberries (optional)

1. Heat oven to 325°F. In medium bowl, combine cookie crumbs, ¼ cup sugar, ½ teaspoon cinnamon and butter; mix until well blended. Press crumb mixture into bottom and up sides of 9-inch springform pan. Bake 8 to 10 minutes. Remove from oven; cool.

2. In small saucepan, scald whipping cream over low heat to just below simmering. Remove from heat. Combine 4 oz. chocolate and scalded whipping cream; mix with wire whisk until blended. Set aside.

3. In large mixing bowl, combine cream cheese, 1 cup sugar, cocoa and ½ teaspoon cinnamon; beat at medium speed until blended. Add egg yolks, one at a time, mixing well after each addition. Blend in 1 teaspoon vanilla and reserved whipping cream mixture; set aside. In clean mixing bowl, combine cream of tartar and egg whites; beat at high speed until soft peaks form. Fold egg whites into cream cheese mixture. Pour into crust; bake 45 to 50 minutes or until center is almost set. Remove from oven; loosen cake from sides of pan. Cool completely before removing rim of pan. Chill several hours or overnight.

4. In small saucepan, scald ¼ cup cream over low heat to just below simmering. Remove from heat. In large mixing bowl, combine 2 oz. chocolate, scalded cream and 1 teaspoon vanilla; mix with wire whisk until blended. Cover; chill until firm but not hard. Using electric mixer, beat chocolate mixture until light and fluffy. Fold in whipped cream. Spread on top of chilled cheesecake and garnish with chocolate curls, almonds or strawberries, if desired. Store in refrigerator.

12 servings.

Preparation time: 45 minutes. Ready to serve: 4 hours.

Per serving: 490 calories, 35 g total fat (20 g saturated fat), 140 mg cholesterol, 250 mg sodium, 2.5 g fiber.

RASPBERRY CREAM CHEESECAKE

Raspberries and chocolate are a perennial top flavor duo on the dessert scene. This no-bake cheesecake makes a refreshing end to any spring menu.

CRUST
- 1½ cups finely crushed chocolate wafers
- ⅓ cup butter or margarine, melted
- ¼ cup sugar

FILLING
- 1 (10-oz.) pkg. frozen raspberries in syrup
- ½ pint fresh raspberries, plus additional for garnish
- 1 (¼-oz.) envelope unflavored gelatin
- ⅔ cup water
- 2 (8-oz.) pkg. cream cheese, softened
- ⅓ cup sugar
- 1 (14-oz.) can sweetened condensed milk
- 1 teaspoon vanilla
- 1 cup whipped cream

TOPPING
- 2 tablespoons almond flavored liqueur
- 1 cup whipped cream
- ¾ cup chocolate ice cream topping

GARNISH
- Fresh mint (optional)
- Fresh raspberries (optional)

❶ Heat oven to 350°F.

❷ In medium bowl, combine crushed chocolate wafers, butter and ¼ cup sugar; mix until blended. Press crumb mixture into bottom and up sides of 9-inch springform pan. Bake 8 to 10 minutes. Remove from oven; cool.

❸ In food processor or blender, process frozen and fresh raspberries until pureed; set aside. In small saucepan, sprinkle gelatin over water; let stand 1 minute. Over low heat, stir until gelatin is dissolved. Remove from heat, set aside.

❹ In mixing bowl, combine cream cheese and ⅓ cup sugar; beat at medium speed until well blended. Gradually beat in sweetened condensed milk; add raspberry puree and vanilla, mixing until blended. Blend in gelatin mixture. Fold in 1 cup whipped cream. Pour mixture into crust; chill until set.

❺ Fold liqueur into 1 cup whipped cream. Top each serving with 1 tablespoon of the chocolate topping and whipped cream. Garnish with mint and fresh raspberries, if desired. Store in refrigerator.

12 servings.

Preparation time: 40 minutes. Ready to serve: 8 hours, 50 minutes.

Per serving: 520 calories, 29.5 g total fat (18 g saturated fat), 90 mg cholesterol, 295 mg sodium, 2.5 g fiber.

LEMON LITE CHEESECAKE DESSERT

This cheesecake offers delicate lemon flavor minus some of the calories of more standard cheesecakes.

CRUST
- 1 cup graham cracker crumbs
- 3 tablespoons butter or margarine, melted
- 1 tablespoon sugar
- 2 teaspoons water
- 1/4 teaspoon grated lemon peel

FILLING
- 10 oz. cream cheese, softened
- 1/4 cup half-and-half
- 1/4 cup powdered sugar
- 1/2 cup lemon sorbet, softened
- 6 oz. lemon flavored yogurt
- 1 teaspoon lemon juice
- 1/2 teaspoon grated lemon peel

TOPPING
- 1 pint strawberries, sliced
- 3 tablespoons sugar

1. Heat oven to 350°F. In medium bowl, combine graham cracker crumbs, butter, 1 tablespoon sugar, water and 1/4 teaspoon lemon peel; mix until well blended. Press into bottom and up sides of 9-inch springform pan. Bake 10 to 12 minutes; cool.

2. In mixing bowl, beat cream cheese at low speed until smooth. Gradually blend in half-and-half; mix at high speed until well blended. Blend in powdered sugar at high speed until mixture becomes light. Place sorbet in separate bowl; fold in cream cheese mixture, yogurt, lemon juice and 1/4 teaspoon lemon peel. Pour mixture into crust, spreading evenly. Cover and freeze until mixture is firm.

3. In medium bowl, combine strawberries and 3 tablespoons sugar; mix lightly. Chill. Serve fruit over dessert. Store in refrigerator.

12 servings.

Preparation time: 40 minutes. Ready to serve: 3 hours, 50 minutes.

Per serving: 190 calories, 12 g total fat (7 g saturated fat), 35 mg cholesterol, 135 mg sodium, 1 g fiber.

CHEF'S NOTES:
- Add 1 or 2 drops yellow food color, if desired.
- Substitute fresh raspberries for strawberries, if desired.

COOKIES

Cookies offer a wide and wonderful world that stretches far, far beyond the home base known as "chocolate chip." Of course, you'll find variations of old favorite cookies here ... and also plenty of new and exciting ideas celebrating the sweet and versatile treats we know as cookies.

Chocolate Espresso Pistachio Wedges, page 66

$\mathcal{E}$SSENTIALS — COOKIES

Cookies are the littlest of cakes — sweet, versatile treats that usually seem to evoke warm memories of childhood, like watching Grandma in her apron at the kitchen stove, baking batches of her own special recipe. But, cookies are not only reserved for the traditional. Some are delicate and lacy and special enough to be served on the finest silver platter. Whatever your preference, the recipes to come will please everyone.

Here you will find Crispy White and Dark Chocolate Chippers (page 72), *the perfect companion to a tall, cool glass of milk, or* Inside Out Fig Bars (page 73), *an updated version of the retro favorite, Fig Newtons, that finds the ooey-gooey center of the cookie on top of a crunchy, cake-like crust.* Double Caramel Tuiles (page 77) *are delicate, lacey and crunchy — the perfect completion to the finest gourmet meal.* Coconut Tea Cakes (page 71) *build from the standard holiday favorite and are delicate, yet crunchy with coconut and toasted pecans.*

Whether it is the memory of cookies and milk for an afternoon snack, the thought of freshly baked Ultimate Oatmeal Raisin Cookies (page 67) *in the lunch box, or as a light yet fancy after dinner treat, cookies are definitely an all-American comfort food. Whatever memories of the word "cookie" come to mind, the recipes in this chapter are sure to please young and old alike.*

INGREDIENTS

Most cookie recipes include common ingredients. Even in the fanciest of cookies, ingredients are commonly found in most kitchen pantries, making an easy dessert even easier to make.

BUTTER. I prefer softened butter for the cookie recipes in this chapter.

BAKING SODA. Baking soda causes baked goods to rise by combining with acid ingredients such as buttermilk, sour milk or yogurt so that carbon dioxide bubbles are released.

BAKING POWDER. This leavening agent is usually made up of baking soda, cream of tartar and a moisture absorber such as cornstarch. Store in a cool, dry place.

CHOCOLATE CHIPS. Freeze chocolate chips before baking to help them retain their shape in the oven.

FLOUR. I use all-purpose flour in these recipes. It comes unbleached and bleached, and can be used interchangeably.

LIQUIDS. The perfect amount of liquid in a cookie dough is a delicate balance. Liquids such as milk or water provide steam, which makes the cookie puff. However, adding too much liquid will thin the batter and cause the cookie to spread.

NUTS. A simple rule to follow: Purchase nuts as fresh as possible. Store them air-tight in a cool place.

SHORTENING. Vegetable shortening can be substituted for other fats in baking. Store at room temperature up to one year.

SUGAR. White sugar or granulated sugar is the most common form of sugar for cooking. It is also the basic table sugar.

VANILLA. Vanilla extract is the most common form of vanilla used today. It is available in supermarkets. Vanilla beans can be found in most specialty stores.

TOOLS

These are just some of the kitchen tools you should have on hand for cookie making (and baking) success.

SPATULA. Use to remove warm cookies from cookie sheets.

WIRE RACKS. Use to cool cookies and stop the cooking process that continues when cookies are left on a hot cookie sheet.

COOKIE SHEETS. Bake on these sheets.

DRY MEASURING CUPS. Use to measure ingredients such as sugar or flour.

ELECTRIC MIXER. Use for quick and effective mixing of ingredients.

LIQUID MEASURING CUPS. Measure ingredients such as milk or water in liquid measuring cups.

MEASURING SPOONS. Accurately measure small amounts of ingredients with these spoons.

MIXING BOWLS. Good, big bowls are necessary for mixing cookie ingredients.

TIMER. A timer ensures accurate doneness.

WOODEN OR PLASTIC SPOONS. These spoons are for mixing or stirring by hand.

TERMS AND TECHNIQUES

Here are some common terms and techniques you'll see in this chapter's cookie recipes.

DROP. To allow batter to fall, without forming it, from a spoon or measuring utensil onto a baking sheet.

CREAM. To mix one or more foods together, usually with an electric mixer, until smooth and fluffy.

CUT IN. To distribute and chop into smaller pieces by using a pastry blender or fork until coarsely divided.

DRIZZLE. To pour liquid in a fine stream over the food.

CHILL. To refrigerate until cold and in some cases until firm in texture.

FOLD. To combine ingredients by gently sliding a spatula or a spoon across the bottom of a mixing bowl and up the side to turn the mixture over, to gently mix without incorporating excess air.

LINE. To cover the bottom of a baking sheet with aluminum foil, parchment paper or waxed paper.

MIX. The combining of several ingredients to evenly disperse them.

PARCHMENT PAPER. A paper resistant to grease and heat, used to line cookie sheets or pans.

TIPS AND INSIGHTS

Here are some tips you'll find educational and fun... and great for making great cookies!

- Always measure a dry ingredient, such as flour, by spooning it into a dry measuring cup and then leveling it off with a straight-edge, such as a ruler or back of a butter knife.

- Always measure liquids, such as water or milk, in a liquid measuring cup and look at the measurement line at eye level for accuracy.

- Bananas are soft and sweet for baking when they are ripe and slightly brown.

- Microwave chocolate in a glass bowl on High for 1 to 2 minutes or until it is almost completely melted. Then stir until smooth.

- If using a rolling pin to roll cookie dough, dust the dough lightly with flour to prevent it from sticking.

- Re-roll cookie dough as little as possible. Rolling the dough more than necessary makes cookie dough tough and chewy.

- To prevent a cookie cutter from sticking to the dough, dip the cutter in flour before making each cut.

- For fewer scraps when cutting cookie dough, start cutting on the outside edge and work your way toward the center.

- Instead of dropping with a spoon, use a small ice cream scoop to easily drop cookies onto cookie sheets.

- Try to make all cookies from one batch the same size, to ensure uniform baking.

- Line cookie sheets with parchment paper for easy removal of cookies after baking. This also saves time on cleanup after a busy day of baking.

- Cookies tend to darken quickly on dark coated cookie sheets; keep this in mind when baking.

- Always be sure to bake cookies in the center of the oven to get the most accurate baking time. If baking more than one sheet, place oven racks so that the oven is divided into thirds.

- Be sure to rotate baking sheets from the top to the bottom shelves when the cookies start to brown, to get a more accurate doneness.

- If you do not have a pastry bag, use a resealable plastic bag with a tiny hole cut in its end to drizzle coconut, nuts, chocolate or caramel onto cookies.

- Sprinkle confectioners' sugar onto warm cookies to help it stick to the cookie.

- Always remove the cookie from the baking sheet when *slightly* cooled, unless the recipe states otherwise. This stops the cookie from continuing to bake on a hot sheet.

- For easier removal when removing cookies from pans such as miniature tartlet pans, use the tip of a thin bladed knife dipped in oil.

- Always be sure to cool cookies completely before storing them or they will get soft and sticky.

- Freeze cookies, tightly wrapped in airtight containers, for up to one month.

CHOCOLATE ESPRESSO PISTACHIO WEDGES

These wedges combine the best of shortbread and sugar cookies. Dipped in fine dark chocolate with a slight hint of espresso, then topped with finely chopped pistachios, these cookies go like heaven with a hot cup of coffee or tea. These cookies are also pictured on pages 60-61.

3   eggs
1   tablespoon finely grated lemon peel
2   teaspoons vanilla
1   cup sugar
3   cups all-purpose flour
½   teaspoon baking powder
¼   teaspoon salt
1   cup (2 sticks) butter, cut into pieces
2   oz. bittersweet chocolate, finely chopped
1   tablespoon instant espresso coffee
¼   cup pistachios, chopped

① In large bowl, beat eggs at high speed about 4 minutes or until slightly thickened. Add lemon peel and vanilla; reduce speed to medium. Slowly add sugar; mix until combined.

② In medium bowl, mix together flour, baking powder and salt. Using pastry blender or fork, cut butter into dry ingredients until mixture crumbles. Stir dry ingredients into wet ingredients until well mixed.

③ Refrigerate dough 2 hours or overnight. Heat oven to 350°F. Roll ¼ of dough into ¼-inch-thick round on lightly floured surface. Refrigerate remaining dough. Cut round into 12 pie-shaped wedges. Repeat with remaining dough.

④ Place wedges on ungreased baking sheets; bake one sheet at a time 8 to 12 minutes or until cookies are light golden brown. Cool slightly; transfer to wire rack to cool completely.

⑤ Place chocolate in small microwave-safe bowl; microwave on High 1 minute or until chocolate is almost melted. Stir until smooth. Stir in ground espresso. Place pistachios in small bowl. Dip large end of each cookie into melted chocolate, then pistachios. Place on cookie sheet lined with parchment paper until set. Transfer to serving plate.

4 dozen cookies.

Preparation time: 2 hours, 30 minutes. Ready to serve: 4 hours, 30 minutes.

Per serving: 95 calories, 5 g total fat (3 g saturated fat), 25 mg cholesterol, 50 mg sodium, 1 g fiber.

ULTIMATE OATMEAL RAISIN COOKIES

No one can resist a delicious and wholesome oatmeal raisin cookie. The cookies here are made the old-fashioned way, the way Grandma used to make them.

1 cup sugar
1 cup water
¾ cup dark raisins
¾ golden raisins
2 eggs
1 cup butter-flavored shortening
1 teaspoon vanilla
2 cups all-purpose flour
2 cups old-fashioned rolled oats
1 teaspoon baking soda
1 teaspoon cinnamon

1 In medium saucepan, bring sugar, water, dark raisins and golden raisins to a boil over medium-high heat; reduce heat. Cover pan; cook 10 minutes. Remove from heat; cool about 40 minutes or until warm to the touch.

2 Heat oven to 350°F. Spray baking sheets with nonstick cooking spray.

3 In large bowl, beat eggs at medium-high speed until slightly thickened. Add shortening and vanilla; continue beating until well mixed.

4 In separate bowl, mix flour, oats, baking soda and cinnamon; slowly add dry ingredients to wet ingredients until combined. Stir in raisin mixture. Drop by rounded tablespoonfuls onto baking sheets. Bake 10 to 14 minutes or until lightly golden brown.

3 dozen cookies.

Preparation time: 1 hour, 15 minutes. Ready to serve: 2 hours.

Per serving: 140 calories, 6.5 g total fat (1.5 g saturated fat), 10 mg cholesterol, 40 mg sodium, 1 g fiber.

DOUBLE CHOCOLATE CONFETTI COOKIES

Think of the richest, gooiest chocolate cookies you ever had. These are better! You'll find your favorite cookie ingredients here — chocolate chips, miniature candy-coated chocolate pieces and coconut — creating a colorful twist on the traditional chocolate chip cookie.

1¼	cups chocolate graham cracker crumbs
1	cup all-purpose flour
2	teaspoons baking powder
1	(14-oz.) can sweetened condensed milk
½	cup shortening
½	cup miniature chocolate chips
½	cup miniature candy-coated chocolate pieces
½	cup white chocolate baking pieces
½	cup flaked coconut
1	cup chopped walnuts

1. Heat oven to 375°F. In medium bowl, combine graham cracker crumbs, flour and baking powder. In large bowl, combine sweetened condensed milk and shortening; beat at medium speed until smooth and creamy. Add dry ingredients to wet ingredients; mix until combined. Fold in chocolate chips, candy-coated pieces, white chocolate pieces, coconut and walnuts.

2. For each cookie, drop 2 level measuring tablespoons of dough into a mound, 3 inches apart, on lightly greased baking sheets. Bake 12 to 14 minutes or until cookies are light golden brown. Cool slightly; remove to wire rack to cool completely.

2½ dozen cookies.

Preparation time: 1 hour, 30 minutes. Ready to serve: 1 hour, 45 minutes.

Per serving: 185 calories, 11 g total fat (4 g saturated fat), 5 mg cholesterol, 70 mg sodium, 1 g fiber.

OLD-TIME CINNAMON BANANA CAKES

These cake-like cookies will please any and every discerning cookie lover, when paired with a tall, cool glass of milk. You'll find these little cakes reminiscent of banana bread and old-time cinnamon snickerdoodles.

1/2	cup (1 stick) butter, softened
1/4	cup butter-flavored shortening
1 1/4	cups sugar
1	egg
1	medium ripe banana, mashed
3/4	cup buttermilk
1	teaspoon vanilla
2 1/4	cups all-purpose flour
1/2	teaspoon baking soda
1/2	teaspoon salt
1 1/2	teaspoons ground cinnamon

1. In large bowl, beat butter, shortening and 1 cup of the sugar at medium speed 3 to 4 minutes or until light and fluffy; mix in egg, banana, buttermilk and vanilla until well blended.

2. In separate bowl, stir together flour, baking soda and salt. Slowly add dry ingredients to wet ingredients; mix well. Refrigerate dough 2 hours or overnight. Stir together remaining 1/4 cup sugar and cinnamon.

3. Heat oven to 400°F; spray baking sheets with nonstick cooking spray.

4. Drop dough by rounded teaspoonfuls onto baking sheets; sprinkle with cinnamon-sugar mixture. Bake 10 to 13 minutes or until set but not brown. Cool slightly; transfer to wire rack to cool completely.

6 dozen (2-inch) cookies.

Preparation time: 2 hours. Ready to serve: 4 hours.

Per serving: 50 calories, 2 g total fat (1 g saturated fat), 6.5 mg cholesterol, 35 mg sodium, 0 g fiber.

COCONUT TEA CAKES

These sweet little treats are a traditional holiday favorite. They're simple to make, too.

- 1 cup (2 sticks) butter, softened
- 1 cup powdered sugar
- 2 teaspoons vanilla
- 2 cups all-purpose flour
- 2/3 cup pecans, toasted, finely chopped*
- 2 cups flaked coconut

1. Heat oven to 350°F.
2. In large bowl, beat butter, 1/2 cup of the powdered sugar and vanilla at medium-high speed 3 to 4 minutes or until fluffy and creamy. Gradually beat in flour and pecans; stir in coconut.
3. Roll dough into 1 1/4-inch balls; place on ungreased baking sheets. Bake 13 to 15 minutes or until slightly golden brown on bottoms. Cool slightly.
4. Place remaining 1/2 cup powdered sugar in small bowl; roll each slightly warm cookie in sugar. Transfer to wire rack to cool completely. Roll each cookie once more in remaining powdered sugar.

3 dozen cookies.

Preparation time: 15 minutes. Ready to serve: 2 hours.

Per serving: 125 calories, 9.5 g total fat (6 g saturated fat), 15 mg cholesterol, 35 mg sodium, 1 g fiber.

TIP *To toast pecans, spread on baking sheet; bake at 375°F for 7 to 10 minutes or until lightly browned. Cool.

CRISPY WHITE AND DARK CHOCOLATE CHIPPERS

These chocolate chip cookies are the perfect all-American sweet treat, made the way chocolate cookies were meant to be made. Crispy, light and extra gooey, they contain milk chocolate and white chocolate. These cookies won't last long in the cookie jar!

1 cup sugar
1 cup packed light brown sugar
1 cup (2 sticks) butter or margarine
2 eggs
1 cup vegetable oil
2 teaspoons vanilla
4 cups all-purpose flour
4 teaspoons cream of tartar
2 teaspoons baking soda
1 teaspoon salt
1½ cups milk chocolate chips
1½ cups white chocolate chips

① Heat oven to 350°F. Spray baking sheets with nonstick cooking spray.

② In large bowl, beat sugar, brown sugar and butter at medium-high speed until light and fluffy. Mix in eggs until blended; pour in oil and vanilla.

③ In separate bowl, combine flour, cream of tartar, baking soda and salt; stir dry ingredients into wet ingredients until well mixed. Fold in milk chocolate chips and white chocolate chips.

④ Drop dough by rounded tablespoonfuls, at least 2 inches apart, on baking sheets; bake 12 to 15 minutes or until lightly browned. Cool slightly; transfer to wire rack to cool completely.

6 dozen (3-inch) cookies.

Preparation time: 1 hour. Ready to serve: 2 hours.

Per serving: 135 calories, 8 g total fat (4 g saturated fat), 15 mg cholesterol, 95 mg sodium, 0 g fiber.

ℐNSIDE-OUT FIG BARS

Remember that old favorite the Fig Newton? A version of this retro favorite, these cookies offer an ooey-gooey fig center "filling" that tops a crunchy, cake-like crust. To finish it off, these bars are sprinkled lightly with powdered sugar.

FILLING
  - 1 cup dried figs
  - ¼ cup almonds
  - ¼ cup raisons
  - ¼ cup apricot preserves
  - ½ teaspoon ground cinnamon

DOUGH
  - 2 cups all-purpose flour
  - ¼ cup sugar
  - ¾ teaspoon baking powder
  - ½ teaspoon salt
  - ½ cup (1 stick) butter
  - 2 eggs

TOPPING
  - ¼ cup powdered sugar

1. Heat oven to 350°F. Line baking sheets with parchment paper.

2. In food processor, pulse figs, almonds and raisins until mixture crumbles. Add preserves and cinnamon; pulse until combined. Set aside.

3. In large mixing bowl, combine flour, sugar, baking powder and salt. Using pastry blender or fork, cut butter into dry ingredients. Beat in eggs at medium speed until dough forms a ball on paddle.

4. Roll ¼ of dough at a time on lightly floured surface to ¼-inch thick. Cut 12 (2-inch) circles from dough. Top each circle with rounded ½ teaspoonful filling. Re-roll dough to cut more circles if necessary. Repeat with remaining dough and filling. Place cookies on baking sheets.

5. Bake one sheet at a time 12 to 15 minutes or until bottoms of cookies are golden brown. Cool slightly; sprinkle with powdered sugar. Transfer to wire rack to cool completely.

4 dozen cookies.

Preparation time: 30 minutes. Ready to serve: 2 hours.

Per serving: 70 calories, 2.5 g total fat (1 g saturated fat), 15 mg cholesterol, 405 mg sodium, 1 g fiber.

APRICOT ALMOND TARTLET COOKIES

These petite shortbread tartlet cookies are filled with a rich and creamy apricot-almond filling that hints of lemon. These tartlets are fancy enough to serve at weddings or showers. Or, wrapped in tissue, they make a perfectly romantic picnic dessert.

½	cup heavy cream
½	cup plus 1 tablespoon sugar
¾	cup dried apricots, chopped
½	cup toasted sliced almonds*
2	teaspoons finely grated lemon peel
½	cup (1 stick) butter, softened
2	teaspoons vanilla
⅛	teaspoon salt
1	cup all-purpose flour

1. Heat oven to 350°F. Generously spray 24 mini-muffin cups with nonstick cooking spray.

2. In medium, heavy-bottomed saucepan, combine cream and ½ cup of the sugar; bring to a full boil over medium-high heat. Remove from heat; stir in apricots, almonds and lemon peel. Set aside.

3. In mixing bowl, beat butter, remaining 1 tablespoon sugar, vanilla and salt at medium-high speed 2 to 3 minutes or until light and fluffy. Add flour; beat until just combined.

4. Divide dough into 24 equal pieces; firmly press 1 piece into bottom and ¼ of the way up sides of each muffin cup. Spoon equal amounts of apricot filling into each cup.

5. Bake 23 to 30 minutes or until cookies are golden brown and filling is bubbly. Let cool 20 to 25 minutes; carefully remove from pan using tip of a small knife to help loosen from edges of cup.

24 cookies.

Preparation time: 1 hour. Ready to serve: 2 hours.

Per serving: 110 calories, 6.5 g total fat (3.5 g saturated fat), 15 mg cholesterol, 40 mg sodium, 1 g fiber.

TIP *To toast almonds, place on baking sheet; bake at 375°F for 6 minutes or until deep golden brown.

*N*UTTY HONEY CHOCOLATE TWISTS

These cookies taste like scones and are filled with chocolate ganache. They also offer a hint of honey and toasted almonds. Their fancy twisted and knotted shape — with ganache filling peeking over the edges — makes them unique and tasty, and is sure to be a hit at any get-together.

DOUGH
- 2 cups all-purpose flour
- ¼ cup sugar
- ¾ teaspoon baking powder
- ½ teaspoon salt
- ½ cup (1 stick) butter
- 2 eggs

FILLING
- ½ cup unblanched almonds, toasted*
- 3 oz. semisweet chocolate, chopped
- ¼ cup honey
- ¼ teaspoon ground cinnamon
- ¼ teaspoon nutmeg

1 Heat oven to 350°F. In large mixing bowl, combine flour, sugar, baking powder and salt. Using pastry blender or fork, cut butter into dry ingredients until mixture crumbles. Beat in eggs, one at a time, with paddle attachment of electric mixer about 1 to 2 minutes or until dough forms into a ball on paddle. Wrap dough in plastic wrap; set aside.

2 In food processor, pulse almonds and chocolate until mixture crumbles. Add honey, cinnamon and nutmeg; pulse until combined.

3 Cut dough into fourths; place ¼ on lightly floured surface. Cover remaining dough with plastic wrap. Roll dough into ¼-inch-thick round. Spread ¼ of chocolate mixture on center of round to within ½ inch of edges. Roll up jelly-roll fashion. Cut in half lengthwise; cut in half lengthwise again. Cut each piece in half horizontally. Twist each piece end-over-end to cross over. Repeat with remaining dough.

4 Bake on ungreased baking sheets one sheet at a time 10 to 15 minutes or until edges are golden brown. Cool slightly; transfer to wire rack to cool completely.

32 cookies.

Preparation time: 30 minutes. Ready to serve: 2 hours, 30 minutes.

Per serving: 100 calories, 5 g total fat (2.5 g saturated fat), 20 mg cholesterol, 75 mg sodium, .5 g fiber.

TIP *To toast almonds, place on baking sheet; bake at 375°F for 6 minutes or until deep golden brown.

DOUBLE CARAMEL CITRUS TUILES

The ultimate in elegance, Double Caramel Citrus Tuiles *prove that cookies really can be a fancy dessert. Delicate, lacy and crunchy, these treats end even the finest gourmet meal magnificently.*

1/2   cup heavy whipping cream
1/4   cup (1/2 stick) butter, cut into pieces
1/4   teaspoon vanilla
3/4   cup coarsely ground almonds
2/3   cup sugar
 2   tablespoons plus 1 teaspoon all-purpose flour
 1   tablespoon finely grated orange peel
 1   tablespoon finely grated lemon peel
1/4   cup caramel sauce

1. In small, heavy-bottomed saucepan, heat cream and butter over medium-high heat, stirring occasionally, until butter is completely melted. Remove from heat; stir in vanilla.

2. In medium mixing bowl, combine almonds, sugar, flour, orange peel and lemon peel; add cream mixture. Stir until well combined. Swirl 2 tablespoons of the caramel sauce into batter. Cover batter tightly with plastic wrap; refrigerate overnight.

3. Heat oven to 325°F; line baking sheets with parchment paper.

4. Drop batter onto baking sheets by teaspoonfuls 1 1/2 inches apart. Bake 8 to 12 minutes or until light golden brown and bubbly. Let cool just long enough to handle; drape hot cookie over rolling pin or edges of narrow rounded glasses. Let sit a few seconds, long enough for cookie to hold its shape; gently roll edges together. Place on platter. Drizzle remaining 2 tablespoons caramel sauce over cookies.

40 cookies.

Preparation time: 10 minutes. Ready to serve: 12 hours, 10 minutes.

Per serving: 55 calories, 3.5 g total fat (1.5 g saturated fat), 5 mg cholesterol, 15 mg sodium, 0 g fiber.

CUSTARDS, MOUSSES & PUDDINGS

by John Schumacher

Little has been done to improve the perfection achieved by earlier centuries' chefs with custards, mousses and puddings. But that doesn't mean these dessert specialties are mundane. On the contrary, they're quite exciting and wonderfully rich and tasty.

Bavarian Cream Pie, page 84

79

ESSENTIALS — CUSTARDS, MOUSSES & PUDDINGS

There are some things we have not been able to improve upon in our modern times. Most desserts are among these things. The main diet for the English in the 15th, 16th and 17th centuries was bland and functional except for these sweet desserts. The abundance of milking cows, and the seaports that received sugar from the New World, made puddings, custards and mousses easy to make for the nobility as well as the common man.

I grew up on a small dairy farm in western Minnesota. My mother is Scandinavian and the English dairy desserts are common to many Scandinavians. Sundays bring back the memories of Bavarian Cream Pie (page 84), *custard and other creamy delights for me. And holidays were filled with family and were highlighted with a large trifle for dessert.*

INGREDIENTS

Listed here are the main ingredients you'll need for preparing this chapter's recipes.

EGGS. The recipes in this chapter all use AA extra-large eggs.

BAKING POWDER. It is best to use fresh baking powder for any recipe; therefore, always buy baking powder in the smallest container possible to ensure freshness.

CHOCOLATE. The recipes in this chapter all use high-quality dark chocolate, not milk chocolate.

CORNSTARCH. Cornstarch of any brand is fine for the recipes in this chapter.

CREAM. I prefer heavy cream with a butterfat content of at least 38%. An excellent place to get this is in a specialty store featuring Mexican ingredients. Their standard for cream is 40% to 42%.

FLOUR. The recipes in this chapter all use all-purpose flour. Do not substitute.

NUTMEG. Fresh whole nutmeg berries, ground in a spice grinder or coffee mill, really make a difference in the taste they impart.

POWDERED SUGAR. Powdered sugar of any brand is fine for the recipes in this chapter.

SUGAR. The recipes in this chapter all use granulated sugar (any brand).

VANILLA. Pure vanilla extract is made with 13.35 ounces of vanilla beans per gallon during extraction, and is 35% alcohol. This is the best vanilla you can buy and use.

TOOLS

These tools are available in any large department, discount or culinary specialty store. The main concern with all cooking equipment is sanitation. Make sure everything is clean. Discard any chipped bowls and glassware. Be sure the cords on all your electrical appliances are free of breaks and not frayed.

BLENDER. A countertop blender is an excellent and essential tool for making custards, mousses and puddings. Today's models can liquify, blend, puree, emulsify and grind.

BOWLS. Buy a top-quality set of plastic mixing bowls that are nonporous, unbreakable and dishwasher safe. Some are even suitable for microwaves.

DOUBLE BROILER. This is two pots with one made to fit inside the other. Simply enough, water in the lower pan cooks food in the upper pan.

MEASURING CUPS. As with measuring spoons, I prefer stainless steel measuring cups. Look for the basic set of $1/4$-, $1/3$-, $1/2$- and 1-cup measures.

MEASURING SPOONS. I prefer stainless steel measuring spoons — they won't snap, bend or break. Look for a basic set consisting of $1/4$ teaspoon, $1/2$ teaspoon, 1 teaspoon and 1 tablespoon.

PIE PLATES. Measured from the inside top of the rim to the opposite side, you'll find three standard sizes: 8-, 9-, and 10-inch. You'll also find "deep-dish" pie plate of 3 inches as compared to the regular $1 1/2$ inches deep. I prefer glass pie plates over metal for recipes like the ones that follow.

ELECTRIC HAND MIXER. With this tool, you can control the power of mixing, whipping, beating and blending. You also control cleanup time — hand mixers reduce it.

RUBBER SPATULA. Rubber spatulas are indispensable in the kitchen. Look for flexibility and grip comfort.

SAUCEPOT. A large saucepan with a lid and two handles; available in sizes from 4 to 14 quarts.

SOUFFLE DISH. There's only one — you need a straight side and a flat bottom soufflé dish.

WIRE WHISK. This tool can have as few as two or as many as 20 wires. Flexibility and function of the whisk are determined by the shape of the wire, and how many wires there are, as well as their length, thickness and the material they are made of.

TERMS AND TECHNIQUES

Knowing the terms and techniques defined below will enhance your culinary experience throughout this chapter's recipes.

WHISK. To move quickly and nimbly, to mix or fluff up by or as if by beating with a whisk.

CHILLED. A food that has been refrigerated, usually at a temperature of 30°F to 40°F.

COMBINE. To mix two or more ingredients together until they do not separate.

LET RIPEN IN FREEZER. To age and let the flavors mellow.

PUREE. To process food by mashing, straining or fine chopping into a smooth pulp.

SIMMER. To maintain the temperature of a liquid just below the boiling point.

TO BEAT STIFF. To mix by stirring rapidly and vigorously in a circular motion to incorporate air until the material (often egg whites but occassionally another key ingredient) stands in peaks.

TURN ONTO PLATE. To turn upside down onto a serving plate.

WATER BATH (BAIN-MARIE). A hot water bath used to cook foods gently or to keep cooked foods hot.

TIPS AND INSIGHTS

Here are a few extra hints to guide you to more success in creating delightful custards, mousses and puddings.

- **FOR MOUSSE AU CHOCOLATE.** If you are not fond of rum, use brandy or just omit alcohol. For a butterscotch version, use butterscotch chips instead of chocolate chips. For extra flair, drizzle chocolate and caramel sauces over the whipped cream.

- **FOR LEMON CUSTARD SPONGE.** You may use half-and-half instead of light cream. Make sure the lemon peel has no white membrane, as the white is very bitter. The bowl for egg whites must be clean and free of fat. There also must be no small parts of the yolk with the egg whites, or the whites will not stiffen. Cake flour is a must!

- **FOR CHEF JOHN'S TRIFLE.** Be sure to have all ingredients assembled before starting any recipe. But remember: With a trifle, there are no holds barred; if you like something, add it! Fun additions and substitutions include fresh fruit (without seeds or pits), brownie pieces or pecan pieces. If serving to children, omit sherry. I assemble trifle 2 to 3 hours ahead to let all the flavors meld.

- **FOR MILK POSSET.** Fresh ground nutmeg gives the best results. You may use 2% or whole milk, but posset will not be as rich or tasty. This is a homerun beverage for fall and winter outings.

Custards, Mousses & Puddings **83**

BAVARIAN CREAM PIE

This pie is pictured on pages 78-79. For chocolate cream pie, add $\frac{1}{2}$ cup cocoa powder to the blender step of the Cream Pie Filling. Or, use as a filling with your favorite pastries.

BAVARIAN CREAM FILLING
- 1 cup heavy cream
- 2 tablespoons powdered sugar
- 1 teaspoon vanilla
- $\frac{1}{4}$ teaspoon almond extract
- 3 cups Cream Pie Filling

CREAM PIE FILLING
- $5\frac{1}{2}$ cups half-and-half
- $1\frac{3}{4}$ cups sugar
- 6 egg yolks
- $\frac{3}{4}$ cup plus 2 tablespoons cornstarch
- 2 teaspoons pure vanilla extract
- Dash salt
- 1 tablespoon butter

PIE CRUST
- 4 cups all-purpose flour
- 1 teaspoon salt
- 1 cup shortening
- $\frac{2}{3}$ cup ice water

1. In large chilled bowl, whip cream, powdered sugar, vanilla and almond extract until stiff.

2. In heavy saucepan, heat half-and-half to a simmer. Do not boil. In blender, blend sugar, egg yolks, cornstarch, vanilla and salt at low speed 20 seconds. Remove 1 cup simmering half-and-half; slowly add to blender. Blend about 30 seconds. Slowly add blended whip cream mixture to simmering half-and-half mixture. Stir constantly until liquid comes to a boil. Immediately remove cooked filling to bowl. Add butter; mix to combine. Cover with plastic wrap. Punch 6 holes with toothpick to let steam escape. Chill in refrigerator.

3. Meanwhile, prepare crust. Heat oven to 350°F. In large bowl, combine flour and salt. Cut in shortening, tossing to make marble-size pieces. Add ice water. Lightly toss just enough to make a dough that holds together. Use pastry cloth or dusted board to roll out crust. For pie crusts, prick crust with fork. Gently shake to shrink dough; place in pie plate. Top with second pie plate. Trim excess dough from edges. Place pans in oven upside down (this keeps crusts from blistering and bubbling); bake 15 to 18 minutes or until crust just begins to brown. Fill baked pie crust with filling and desired fruit topping. Store in refrigerator.

8 servings.

4 single- or 2 double- (9-inch) pie crusts.

Preparation time: 35 minutes. Ready to serve: 3 hours, 15 minutes.

Per serving: 440 calories, 27 g total fat (14 g saturated fat), 135 mg cholesterol, 135 mg sodium, .5 g fiber.

MELON AND TAPIOCA PUDDING

Tapioca is made from Cassava root — a large, long starchy root with tough brown skin and crisp white flesh.

  5   lb. ripe watermelon
  1   teaspoon lemon juice
  ¼   cup quick-cooking tapioca
  1   cup sugar
  ½   cup powdered sugar
  ¼   cup cornstarch
  2   cups Sweet Whipped Cream (page 87)

① Remove melon from rind; discard seeds. Cut melon into 1-inch cubes; process in blender just until it is pureed.

② In heavy saucepan, bring melon puree and juice, lemon juice and tapioca to a boil over medium-high heat. Sift together sugar, powdered sugar and cornstarch; stir into boiling liquid. Reduce heat to medium; stir with wooden spoon 2 to 3 minutes.

③ Remove from heat; cool 20 minutes. Spoon mixture in stem glassware; chill 2 to 3 hours. Top with Sweet Whipped Cream.

6 servings.

Preparation time: 15 minutes. Ready to serve: 2 hours, 15 minutes.

Per serving: 405 calories, 14 g total fat (7.5 g saturated fat), 45 mg cholesterol, 20 mg sodium, 1 g fiber.

MILK POSSET

Posset is a drink made from milk that is lightly curdled by adding an acidic liquid such as wine, ale or citrus juice. Posset is sweetened and often spiced. In the Middle Ages, hot milk, wine, sugar and spices (this recipe!) were considered a remedy for colds. Even if it doesn't have curative powers, Milk Posset *is sure to help you feel a little better! For festive occasions, beaten eggs were added to make a rich holiday drink.*

  1   pint half-and-half
  2   tablespoons powdered sugar
 ¹⁄₈ teaspoon salt
 ¹⁄₄ cup sweet sherry, marsala or port wine
Dash ground nutmeg

1. In heavy saucepan, heat half-and-half over medium-low heat about 7 minutes or until mixture comes to a froth. Do not boil.

2. Meanwhile, in separate bowl, combine powdered sugar, salt and wine; whisk until smooth. Slowly whisk mixture into steamy half-and-half. Serve in warmed mugs. Top with nutmeg.

4 mugs.

Preparation time: 5 minutes. Ready to serve: 12 minutes.

Per serving: 195 calories, 14 g total fat (9 g saturated fat), 45 mg cholesterol, 120 mg sodium, 0 g fiber.

ENGLISH TOFFEE MARLOW

Marshmallow is the name of a confection and a plant from Europe and Asia. The mallow plant looks like the hollyhock, and is chiefly grown for its roots. These roots provide the traditional base for the sweet confection known as marshmallow. The toffee presented here is made from syrup cooked to the hard-ball stage, then combined with gelatin and whisked into beaten egg whites. Dust the mixture with icing sugar, let it set and then cut into cubes or rounds.

MARLOW
3	cups half-and-half
1/2	lb. marshmallows
1 1/4	cups Sweet Whipped Cream
1	cup English toffee, crushed

SWEET WHIPPED CREAM
1	pint heavy cream
2	teaspoons vanilla
1/3	cup powdered sugar

1. In double boiler, heat 1/4 cup of the half-and-half with marshmallows. Fold mixture repeatedly until marshmallows are half melted. Remove from heat; continue folding mixture while cooling until it is smooth and fluffy.

2. Fold in remaining 2 3/4 cups half-and-half; freeze in 13x9-inch pan. For cream: in chilled mixing bowl, combine cream, vanilla and powdered sugar; beat at medium speed until cream is thick and holds a peak.

3. Just before freezing, gently stir in whipped cream and 1/2 cup of the toffee. Let mixture freeze 30 minutes. Stir in remaining 1/2 cup toffee. Let ripen in freezer 2 to 3 hours before serving.

6 servings.

Preparation time: 15 minutes. Ready to serve: 3 hours, 30 minutes.

Per serving: 755 calories, 45.5 g total fat (28 g saturated fat), 150 mg cholesterol, 210 mg sodium, 0 g fiber.

Custards, Mouses & Puddings   **87**

MOUSSE AU CHOCOLATE

Mousse *refers to dishes with a foamy texture, usually cold (such as this recipe) or frozen. But in some cases mousse is served warm or hot.*

8 oz. unsweetened chocolate
2 tablespoons heavy cream
1 tablespoon rum
¼ cup (½ stick) butter
½ cup sugar
4 egg yolks
6 egg whites
Whipped cream for garnish (optional)
Chocolate curls or pieces for garnish (optional)

1 Break chocolate into small pieces. Place in top half of double boiler with cream and rum. Heat in double boiler until chocolate is smooth and free of lumps. Cool about 30 minutes or until room temperature.

2 In bowl, beat butter and 6 tablespoons of the sugar at medium speed until pale and fluffy. Beat in egg yolks, one at a time, until smooth.

3 Add cooled melted chocolate to butter mixture; beat 5 minutes at medium speed until light.

4 Using clean bowl and beaters, beat egg whites until foamy. Gradually beat in remaining 2 tablespoons sugar until stiff. Fold beaten egg whites into chocolate base with wire whisk.

5 Spoon mousse into chilled stem glasses; chill until set. Garnish with whipped cream sprinkled with chocolate curls, if desired.

6 servings.

Preparation time: 45 minutes. Ready to serve: 2 hours.

Per serving: 500 calories, 35 g total fat (20 g saturated fat), 205 mg cholesterol, 200 mg sodium, 1.5 g fiber.

RUSSIAN CRANBERRY KISEL

Kisel is an ancient Russian fruit dessert thickened with arrowroot. Meaning "sour," kisel is made with acidic fruits such as gooseberries, cranberries, raspberries, blackberries, rhubarb or oranges. Any fruit may be used, but kisel is best when it features cranberries.

¾   cup apple cider
1   (12-oz.) bag fresh cranberries*
2   tablespoons honey
½   cup sugar
½   cup packed brown sugar
1   tablespoon cornstarch
1   pint heavy cream
¼   cup powdered sugar
1   recipe *Sablée* (page 91)

① In medium saucepan, bring apple cider and cranberries to a slow boil over medium heat. Boil 5 minutes. Stir in honey; combine well.

② Sift together sugar, brown sugar and cornstarch; stir into fruit mixture with wooden spoon. Stir often to keep from scorching. Cook about 3 minutes or until sauce is clear and shiny. (Cranberries will be soft and broken up; sauce will be clear and shiny.) Place in bowl; refrigerate.

③ In medium bowl, whip cream and powdered sugar until stiff. With wire whisk, fold ¾ of chilled cranberry mixture into whipped cream; spoon into stem glasses. Top with remaining puree; chill. Serve with Sablée.

6 servings.

Preparation time: 30 minutes. Ready to serve: 2 hours, 30 minutes.

Per serving: 455 calories, 25 g total fat (15.5 g saturated fat), 90 mg cholesterol, 35 mg sodium, 2.5 g fiber.

TIP *Cranberries grown in Northern Europe are smaller than American cranberries.

SABLEE

Sablée is a French cookie with a delicate, crumbly texture, often flavored with grated citrus peel or almonds. The classic novel, War and Peace, *is the reason for this pairing of Russian and French ingredients. Napoleon spent a great deal of time in Russia, and the Russian aristocracy was enamored by French cuisine. Thus, the melding of two diverse cuisines occurred.*

  1   cup all-purpose flour
 ½   cup (1 stick) butter, cold, cut into cubes
 ½   cup (2 oz.) grated mild white cheddar cheese
  2   tablespoons cold water
  1   egg, whisked smooth
 ¼   teaspoon vanilla
 ⅓   cup pecan pieces*

❶ Heat oven to 350°F.

❷ Place flour in large chilled bowl. Add butter; rub into pea-size pieces. Stir in cheese. Pour in cold water; knead gently 10 times.

❸ On lightly floured pastry cloth, roll crust to form 8-inch square; cut into 4 strips. In small bowl, combine egg and vanilla; brush over strips. Quickly, but carefully, place strips on lightly greased 15x10x1-inch baking sheet. Spread pecans evenly over strips. With fingertips, gently press pecans into dough.

❹ Bake about 20 minutes. Remove Sablée from pan; cool on wire rack.

4 cookies.

Preparation time: 20 minutes. Ready to serve: 35 minutes.

Per serving: 450 calories, 35 g total fat (18 g saturated fat), 100 mg cholesterol, 250 mg sodium, 1.5 g fiber.

TIP *Salted peanuts are delicious instead of pecans.

LEMON CUSTARD SPONGE

Custard is a mixture of eggs and milk or cream thickened by gentle heating. The name is derived from crustade — *a tart with a crust. The French have no word for custard so they use the term* crème.

4 egg yolks
1 tablespoon butter, melted
1½ cups sugar
⅓ cup lemon juice
1 teaspoon grated lemon peel
¼ teaspoon salt
¼ teaspoon ground nutmeg
⅓ cup cake flour, sifted
1 cup light cream
8 egg whites
   Powdered sugar for dusting
   Whipped heavy cream for topping, if desired

❶ Heat oven to 350°F. Butter and flour 2½-quart soufflé dish.

❷ In blender, mix egg yolks, butter and ¾ cup of the sugar at low speed 20 seconds. Mix in lemon juice, lemon peel, salt, nutmeg and flour at low speed 20 seconds. Slowly add cream.

❸ In clean, warm mixing bowl, beat egg whites at medium speed until foamy. Continue beating at high speed, gradually adding remaining ¾ cup sugar until egg whites form stiff peaks. With wire whisk, fold in egg yolk mixture.

❹ Gently pour batter into soufflé dish; set in warm water bath so water is 2 inches up sides of dish. Bake 50 minutes; remove from oven and water bath. Dust top with powdered sugar.

❺ Spoon soft soufflé into warm dish; top with whipped cream.

4 servings.

Preparation time: 25 minutes. Ready to serve: 45 minutes.

Per serving: 375 calories, 13 g total fat (7 g saturated fat), 175 mg cholesterol, 210 mg sodium, 0 g fiber.

PINEAPPLE DATE GINGER UPSIDE DOWN PUDDING

Pudding is difficult to define. It is a cooked dish consisting of various sweet or savory ingredients, or mixed with flour and eggs, served within a flour-based crust.

¼ cup long-grain rice
1 cup half-and-half
⅔ cup butter
3 tablespoons pure maple syrup
⅓ cup sugar
1 (20-oz.) can pineapple rings, drained
9 pitted dates
½ cup packed brown sugar
½ teaspoon ground nutmeg
¼ teaspoon ground cinnamon
2 teaspoons vanilla
2 egg yolks
¾ cup all-purpose flour
2 teaspoons ground ginger
1 teaspoon baking powder
4 egg whites

❶ Heat oven to 350°F. Place rice and half-and-half in shallow baking pan. Cover with aluminum foil; poke 6 pencil-size holes in foil. Bake 40 minutes or until rice is tender and liquid is absorbed. Refrigerate 30 minutes.

❷ Meanwhile, grease and flour 9-inch square pan. In saucepan, melt 2 tablespoons of the butter over low heat. Mix in maple syrup and sugar until smooth. Pour batter into pan. Place pineapple rings 3x3 on bottom of pan with 1 date in center of each ring.

❸ In bowl, whisk remaining butter until smooth. In separate bowl, combine brown sugar, nutmeg, cinnamon and vanilla; whisk into butter until smooth. Whisk in egg yolks until smooth. Stir in cold rice; combine well. Sift together flour, ginger and baking powder; pour over rice mixture. Combine gently as not to crush rice.

❹ In small, clean bowl, beat egg whites until stiff. Fold ⅓ of egg whites into rice mixture. Repeat twice. Evenly top fruit with rice mixture. Bake 35 minutes. Remove from oven; turn out onto serving platter. Serve with whipped cream or ice cream.

9 servings.

Preparation time: 30 minutes. Ready to serve: 65 minutes.

Per serving: 380 calories, 18 g total fat (11 g saturated fat), 95 mg cholesterol, 190 mg sodium, 1.5 g fiber.

CHEF JOHN'S TRIFLE

As far as I'm concerned, trifle is the *dessert of desserts.*

1	angel food cake
6	to 8 vanilla wafers, broken into coarse pieces
1/3	cup sweet sherry
1	cup raspberry jam
1/2	cup peach jam
1/2	cup sliced almonds
4	cups Cream Pie Filling (page 84), chilled
3 1/2	cups Sweet Whipped Cream (page 87)
3	cups fresh or individually quick frozen raspberries
1/2	cup chocolate sauce
1/2	cup caramel sauce
	Chocolate shavings or pieces

❶ Tear cake into walnut-size pieces.

❷ In small bowl, sprinkle vanilla wafers with sherry. In separate bowl, combine raspberry jam and peach jam.

❸ Toast almonds on buttered pan in 350°F oven 5 minutes; cool. Do not toast almonds darker than light brown.

❹ Now the fun part. Layer 1: In clean, well-chilled bowl, layer 1/3 of angel food pieces. Top with 1 1/2 cups cream filling, 1/2 cup jam, 1 cup whipped cream and 1/3 of raspberries. Top with 1/2 of vanilla wafer pieces.

❺ Layer 2: Repeat previous step for next layer; top with 1/2 of chocolate sauce and 1/2 of caramel sauce.

❻ Layer 3: Repeat layering process. Top with almonds. Remember this is the top and it needs to look well designed. Cover with plastic wrap; refrigerate until chilled. Store in refrigerator.

12 servings.

Preparation time: 30 minutes. Ready to serve: 2 hours, 30 minutes.

Per serving: 690 calories, 25 g total fat (13 g saturated fat), 130 mg cholesterol, 520 mg sodium, 3.5 g fiber.

FRUIT DESSERTS

by Michele Anna Jordan

Sometimes simplicity is the best plan. That's what these fruit-based desserts are all about — a light and simple elegance defined by the full and robust flavor of each of the wonderful fruits featured.

Broiled Persimmons with Kiwi and Pomegranates, page 102

ESSENTIALS — FRUIT DESSERTS

A perfect peach, picked at its exact moment of ripeness and peeled — its skin comes off with nothing more than a gentle tug — and eaten right there in the orchard or farmers' market: This is the ideal dessert. Carry the peaches home and present them on individual plates, and you will dazzle your guests with your wisdom and audacity. Even when we can't get fruit at its absolute peak of perfection, fruit desserts offer a delicious conclusion to any meal. Many fruit desserts have the added advantage of simplicity, especially when you choose organically grown fruits in their true season, grown for flavor rather than their ability to withstand long-distance shipping. Fruit desserts also leave you and your guests feeling refreshed rather than too full.

You can, of course, use fruits in rich, indulgent, elaborate desserts too, from fruit fools — simply, fruit purees folded into whipped cream — to strawberry shortcake, peach pie, mango mousse, blueberry ice cream, and raspberry cake with chocolate cream filling. All the recipes here attempt to highlight the simple goodness of the fruit itself.

INGREDIENTS

Selecting good fruit is as important as cooking the desserts in this chapter!

APPLES. Apples should be very firm and crisp, without soft spots and with few blemishes.

BERRIES. Strawberries and other berries are very fragrant when grown and harvested properly; a strawberry without an aroma is not a pleasant berry.

CITRUS. All citrus should feel heavy in your hand and should "give" slightly when gently pressed or squeezed. Rock-hard lemons will not yield much juice; fruits that are too soft may have flavors of decay.

MUSK MELONS (Cantaloupe). There should be just the very slightest give near the stem end of the melon, which should feel heavy in your hand.

PEARS. There are many varieties of pears, some that are soft when ripe, others that remain firm. Unlike most other fruit, pears are best when picked before fully ripe and held in cold storage. To determine when they are ready, gently press the area around the stem; if it gives slightly, it is time to enjoy the pear.

PERSIMMONS. There are two types: The Fuyu, which is ripe when still firm, and the Hachiya, which is very astringent until it is fully ripe.

STONE FRUIT. Stone fruit should be heavy in your hand and fragrant when sniffed close to the skin. Do not squeeze them, as they bruise easily.

WATERMELON. Melons should make a sharp crack when tapped.

SEASONAL GUIDE TO FRUIT

With so much produce coming from the southern hemisphere, it is difficult to remember what is in season when. The best way to know is to shop at a certified farmers' market: Then, all you have to do is look around; if it's at the market, it's in season nearby. If you don't have a farmers' market, talk to the produce manager of your favorite store about what produce may come from your region's growers.

Early Spring Fruits — Strawberries, Rhubarb, Pears.

Late Spring Fruits — Apricots, Early Peaches, Bing Cherries, Blueberries.

Summer Fruits — Raspberries, Blackberries, Olallieberries, White Peaches, Nectarines, Plums, Gravenstein Apples, Watermelon, Charentais Melon, Cantaloupe, Crenshaw Melon, Crane Melon, Sharlyn Melon, Queen Anne Cherries, Papaya, Mango, Currants.

Fall Fruits — Apples, Pears, Figs, Pomegranates, Cranberries, Grapes, Blood Peaches.

Winter Fruits — Kiwifruit, Persimmons, Pears, Quince, Grapefruit, Oranges, Blood Oranges, Tangerines, Meyer Lemons.

TOOLS

Obviously, you need nothing special to serve a bowl of peaches or apricots, or a wedge of crisp watermelon. In general, the preparation of fruit desserts requires little in the way of special equipment; you likely have everything you need (see below) in your kitchen already.

BALLOON WHISK. Choose a sturdy one; it is the best tool for whipping cream and egg whites by hand.

DOUBLE BOILER. If you use this cooking method frequently, you should purchase a good double boiler. If you use it only frequently, you can make do with a medium saucepan and a stainless steel bowl that rests on the rim of the pan.

FOOD MILL. A food mill purees cooked fruits without introducing air, as a food processor or blender does.

HEAVY-DUTY RUBBER SPATULAS. Le Crueset makes a line of colorful rubber spatulas that withstand high heat and do not crack as the old white rubber spatulas do. These "newfangled" spatulas come in a variety of widths, all of which are handy to use.

IMMERSION BLENDER. This is a hand-held electric wand that is immersed directly into the food to be pureed. It introduces less air than a traditional blender, and is very easy to use.

NONREACTIVE SAUCEPANS. When working with fruit, do not use cast iron or aluminum, both of which can react with the fruit's acid and create off flavors, off colors and metallic tastes.

NUTMEG GRINDER. The best way to grate whole nutmeg is with a hand-cracked nutmeg grinder, a tool that looks like a peppermill. Insert a whole nutmeg into the bottom of the grinder, put the blade closure in place, and turn the hand crank on the top to shave off slices so thin that they turn to powder immediately.

PARING KNIFE. Good knives are always worth the investment. Choose a forged blade rather than a stamped one, test the handles to discover which is most comfortable in your hand, and if you don't know, ask the salesperson to show you the necessary techniques for maintaining a sharp blade.

WOODEN SPOONS. Selecting spoons with substantial handles — larger than the common spindly ones — will allow you to stir for several minutes without your hand growing tired.

TERMS AND TECHNIQUES

Review these terms and techniques before re-creating this chapter's recipes.

CITRUS ZEST. Zest refers to the thinnest outer layer of a citrus fruit, the part that contains not just the color but most of the essential oils. Before removing it, rinse the fruit in warm running water and dry it thoroughly. To use a microplane zest, rub the fruit back and forth over the blade, turning the fruit constantly as you do. To use a conventional zester, which looks similar to a paring knife but has a short flat blade with several sharp holes, scrape the blade over the surface of the fruit, removing as thin a strip of zest as possible with each scrape. To use a vegetable peeler, hold it gently and try to avoid any of the bitter white pith that lies beneath the zest. Do not use a standard cheese grater; although most have a zesting blade, they are inefficient and you will usually end up with grated knuckles.

SIMPLE SYRUP. Also known as bar sugar or bar syrup because it is used to sweeten mixed drinks, it is a mixture of two parts sugar and one part water, simmered over high heat until it is completely transparent. It can be stored in the refrigerator indefinitely.

TO EXTRACT THE SEEDS OF A POMEGRANATE. Cut a pomegranate in half, hold it over a bowl to catch the juices, and use your fingers to remove the seeds one section at a time.

TO MAKE CITRUS SEGMENTS. Hold a peeled citrus fruit in the palm of one hand; hold that hand over a bowl to catch any juice. Use a sharp knife to cut close to each membrane to loosen the segment, which will slip out easily.

TO MAKE CREME FRAICHE. Wash a tablespoon, measuring cup and clean glass bowl or crock in very hot water. Pour two cups of heavy cream into the bowl, stir in 1 tablespoon buttermilk, cover with a clean plate or clean tea towel, and set in a warm place until the mixture thickens, about 24 hours. If you don't have time to make true crème fraîche, you can mix together equal amounts of sour cream and half-and-half or heavy cream.

To peel citrus. Slice off both ends of the fruit, cutting down to the flesh. Set the fruit upright on a work surface and hold it steady with one hand. With the other hand, use a very sharp knife to cut off the peel down to the flesh, cutting downward and following the curve of the fruit as you cut.

TIPS AND INSIGHTS

Follow these tips and you will find much success with the fruit recipes that follow.

- If you find yourself with fruit that does not have as much flavor as you'd like, you can sometimes boost that flavor by adding a bit of sugar or simple syrup (page 100). Add 2 or 3 tablespoons of simple syrup to pear soup, for example, when the pears are not at their very best.

- Serve some fresh fruit "dessert appetizers" in cupcake liners.

- Strawberries make their own syrup. Sprinkle clean strawberries with sugar (about 2 to 3 teaspoons per pint) and refrigerate for at least two hours. If the strawberries are a bit too firm and haven't yet developed their full flavor, add twice this amount of sugar.

- The best way to drizzle honey is with a wooden honey wand. The wooden bulb on the end holds the honey, allowing it to drizzle at just the right speed.

- When a dessert recipe calls for a pan to be coated in butter, do not use spray oil in its place. Although the amount — generally a teaspoon or two — may seem negligible, the small amount of butter contributes important flavor and might be crucial in forming the proper texture as well.

BROILED PERSIMMONS WITH KIWI AND POMEGRANATES

Persimmons ripen when we need them most, after trees have dropped their leaves and days have turned gray and gloomy. Then, they hang on their bare branches like colorful jewels. Here persimmons are paired with two of their seasonal companions — like kiwi and pomegranate— for a bright and refreshing dessert. This recipe is also pictured on pages 96-97.

4	ripe Hachiya persimmons
8	teaspoons packed dark brown sugar
4	teaspoons butter, chilled, very thinly sliced
8	firm-ripe kiwi fruit, peeled, chilled
¼	cup crème fraîche, chilled
¾	cup red ripe pomegranate seeds (from 1 large)
8	thin lime wedges

❶ Set broiler rack at least 3 inches from flame or heating coil; heat broiler.

❷ Cut each persimmon in half lengthwise; remove stems. Set persimmon halves on baking sheet cut-side up; sprinkle 2 teaspoons of the brown sugar over each half, covering entire surface of fruit. Top each persimmon with a few thin slices of butter.

❸ Place persimmons under broiler; broil until it's tender when pierced with fork and brown sugar is melted and begins to sizzle, 6 to 8 minutes. Cut kiwi fruit into ¼-inch-thick crosswise slices.

❹ Set 2 persimmon halves on individual dessert plates; arrange kiwi fruit around them. Stir crème fraîche to loosen it; spoon 1 tablespoon over each portion. Scatter pomegranate seeds on top. Garnish each portion with 2 lime wedges; serve immediately.

4 servings.

Preparation time: 25 minutes. Ready to serve 33 minutes.

Per serving: 350 calories, 9.5 g total fat (5 g saturated fat), 25 mg cholesterol, 45 mg sodium, 13 g fiber.

LEMON CURD

Indulge in afternoon tea! Serve this Lemon Curd *in a little dish alongside hot scones.*

3 eggs
2 egg yolks
¾ cup sugar
   Dash salt
   Grated peel of 3 lemons
½ cup fresh lemon juice, strained
½ cup (1 stick) unsalted butter, melted

1. Fill bottom of double boiler half full with water; bring to a boil over medium heat. Reduce heat to low so water simmers slowly.

2. Using top part of double boiler as mixing bowl, beat eggs and egg yolks until smooth and creamy. Mix in sugar, salt and lemon peel. Stir in lemon juice. Slowly mix in butter. Set mixture over simmering water; stir continuously until it just begins to thicken, about 15 minutes. Remove top part of double boiler; set it on cool work surface. As mixture cools, it will gradually thicken. When cooled to about room temperature, pour or spoon it into glass jar. Cover with lid; refrigerate until ready to use.

About 1 pint lemon curd.

Preparation time: 30 minutes. Ready to serve: 45 minutes.

Per serving: 110 calories, 7 g total fat (4 g saturated fat), 80 mg cholesterol, 35 mg sodium, 0 g fiber.

ROASTED STRAWBERRIES WITH VANILLA BEAN ICE CREAM

Wonderful desserts need not be elaborate or difficult. Few things are simpler than these roasted strawberries, but they are absolutely luscious. For a lighter, more delicate version, omit ice cream.

- 8   cups strawberries, stems removed
- ¼   cup vanilla sugar
- 2   tablespoons balsamic vinegar
- 1   pint vanilla bean ice cream, commercial or homemade

① Put strawberries in large colander, rinsing under cool tap water. Shake off most of the water. Slice strawberries ⅛ inch thick. Place them in large bowl; sprinkle with vanilla sugar. Cover; refrigerate at least 1 hour or up to 4 hours.

② Heat oven to 375°F. Toss strawberries with balsamic vinegar; place them, along with their juices, in large ovenproof skillet or baking dish. Bake 8 to 10 minutes or until juices are bubbling and strawberries are hot but not mushy.

③ Divide strawberries among individual soup plates; top each portion with generous scoop or two of vanilla bean ice cream. Serve immediately.

6 servings.

Preparation time: 30 minutes. Ready to serve: 40 minutes.

Per serving: 185 calories, 5.5 g total fat (3 g saturated fat), 19.5 mg cholesterol, 37.5 mg sodium, 4.5 g fiber.

GRILLED STONE FRUIT WITH CHOCOLATE SAUCE

Grilling fruit intensifies its flavor. It is also a great way to use the heat of dying coals. If the weather cooperates, you can enjoy this dessert outside around the fire.

6 ripe apricots, halved, pitted
6 ripe peaches, preferably white, halved, pitted
6 ripe nectarines, halved, pitted
6 oz. bittersweet chocolate, preferably Scharfen Berger, chopped
3 tablespoons half-and-half
2 tablespoons framboise (optional)
1 cup fresh red raspberries

❶ Heat grill.

❷ Fill bottom of double boiler half full with water; bring to a boil over medium heat. Reduce heat to low so water simmers slowly.

❸ Arrange apricots, peaches and nectarines skin-side down on grill rack 4 to 6 inches from medium hot coals. Cook until fruit begins to soften and brown, about 3 to 5 minutes.

❹ Arrange fruit, skin-side down, on serving platter; cover with tea towel to keep hot.

❺ Set top part of double boiler on top of simmering water; add chocolate and half-and-half. When chocolate is melted, stir gently to mix. Slowly add framboise, if using.

❻ Drizzle chocolate sauce over fruit; garnish with raspberries. Serve immediately.

6 servings.

Preparation time: 30 minutes. Ready to serve: 35 minutes.

Per serving: 285 calories, 14 g total fat (7.5 g saturated fat), 5 mg cholesterol, 5 mg sodium, 9 g fiber.

FIGS WITH CHEESE, HONEY AND WALNUTS

Figs generally ripen about the same time summer light takes on the golden hue that signals autumn's approach — around mid to late August.

- 8 fresh ripe figs, cut in half lengthwise
- 1 cup fromage blanc, fresh ricotta cheese or 3/4 cup mascarpone
- 3 tablespoons honey, preferably dark honey, such as lavender
- 1/2 cup shelled walnuts, toasted*

1 Arrange figs on platter or individual serving plates. Place cheese in center of platter or add a generous spoonful to individual plates. Drizzle honey over cheese and figs; add walnuts. Serve immediately.

4 servings.

Preparation time: 10 minutes. Ready to serve: 20 minutes.

Per serving: 310 calories, 16 g total fat (6 g saturated fat), 30 mg cholesterol, 55 mg sodium, 4 g fiber.

TIP *To toast walnuts, spread on baking sheet; bake at 375°F for 7 to 10 minutes or until lightly browned. Cool.

APPLE FRITTERS WITH CINNAMON SUGAR

Serve fruit fritters in the winter, following a hearty soup and a big salad. For a slightly more indulgent version, serve a bowl of crème fraîche (page 100) or sour cream (for dipping) alongside these fritters.

2	eggs, separated
¾	cup buttermilk
1	tablespoon butter, melted
1¼	cups all-purpose flour
2	tablespoons plus ¼ cup sugar
½	teaspoon kosher (coarse) salt
½	teaspoon plus 1 tablespoon ground cinnamon
	Whole nutmeg
3 to 4	sweet-tart apples, peeled, cored, diced (about 2 cups total)
	Peanut oil for frying

❶ In medium mixing bowl, whisk together egg yolks, buttermilk and butter. In separate bowl, combine flour, 2 tablespoons of the sugar, salt, ½ teaspoon of the cinnamon and several gratings of nutmeg. Combine mixtures; let rest, covered, at least 1 hour or up to 3 hours.

❷ Beat egg whites until they form stiff peaks but are not dry; fold into buttermilk batter. Fold in apples. In small bowl, mix remaining ¼ cup sugar and 1 tablespoon cinnamon; set aside.

❸ Pour 3 inches peanut oil into large heavy pot set over medium flame or burner. Heat until oil reaches 370°F. Carefully drop batter by rounded tablespoonfuls into oil, waiting until oil bubbles before adding another spoonful. Work in batches; do not crowd fritters. Cook, turning once, until each fritter is golden brown, about 5 minutes. Transfer to absorbent paper. When fritters are cooling, sprinkle with cinnamon-sugar. Set cloth napkin on plate or in wide basket. Transfer fritters to napkin; serve immediately.

About 2 dozen fritters.

Preparation time: 30 minutes. Ready to serve: 1 hour, 36 minutes.

Per serving: 80 calories, 3.5 g total fat (1 g saturated fat), 20 mg cholesterol, 50 mg sodium, 1 g fiber.

CHILLED PEAR SOUP

Fruit soups are a delightful way to conclude an elegant meal. And because they must be eaten slowly, spoonful by spoonful, they encourage lingering and the conversation that inevitably goes with it. You can serve a wedge of blue cheese — Maytag, Gorgonzola, Pt. Reyes or any French blue — alongside; the tangy cheese is lovely with the sweet and smooth soup.

	Juice of 1 lemon
4 to 6	ripe Comice pears
2 to 4	tablespoons sugar (optional)
2	slices fresh ginger
2	teaspoons black peppercorns
2	cardamom seeds (not pods)
	Dash salt
2½	cups water
1	cup fruity (not sweet) white wine, chilled
2	tablespoons fresh mint leaves, cut into thin strips

1. Fill medium bowl half full with water; stir in lemon juice. Using vegetable peeler or very sharp paring knife, peel pears, setting each one into lemon water after peeling. After all of the pears have been peeled, cut them in half lengthwise; remove seed cores. Cut pears into medium dice, returning them to water so they do not brown. Taste a piece of pear; if it is not fully ripe and sweet, you will need to add sugar in the next step.

2. Drain pears in strainer or colander, shaking off excess water. Place pears in medium saucepan; stir in 2 tablespoons of the sugar, if needed, along with ginger, peppercorns, cardamom seeds, salt and water. Bring to a boil over medium heat; reduce heat to low. Simmer until pears are tender, about 15 minutes. Taste; add more sugar if necessary to boost flavor. Stir until sugar is dissolved; remove from heat. Cool.

3. Use tongs to remove and discard ginger slices. Set food mill or sieve over medium bowl; use slotted spoon to transfer pears to mill or sieve. Grind or press pears, discarding any peppercorns or cardamom seeds left behind. Strain cooking liquid into bowl; discard peppercorns and cardamom seeds. Stir liquid into pureed pears. Chill mixture at least 3 hours or overnight.

4. Stir wine into pear puree. Ladle into soup plates; garnish with mint. Serve immediately.

6 servings.

Preparation time: 40 minutes. Ready to serve: 4 hours, 5 minutes.

Per serving: 125 calories, 1 g total fat (0 g saturated fat), 0 mg cholesterol, 50 mg sodium, 5 g fiber.

PUMPKIN POTS DE CREME

I believe the most important quality in any custard is tenderness, which is achieved here by using just the yolks of eggs. It is also crucial to not cook the custard too long, or it will toughen and break. The peppercorns add a layer of flavor that isn't easily identified but that lingers pleasantly on the palate.

2   cups half-and-half
1/3   cup sugar
      Dash salt
1   tablespoon white peppercorns
1   teaspoon black peppercorns
1/2   teaspoon ground cinnamon
1   cup pumpkin puree
6   egg yolks, lightly beaten

1 In medium saucepan, whisk together half-and-half, sugar and salt. Stir in white and black peppercorns and cinnamon; bring to a boil over medium heat. Reduce heat; simmer, stirring continuously, 10 minutes. Remove from heat. Cover; let steep 30 minutes.

2 Heat oven to 350°F. Whisk pumpkin into half-and-half mixture; strain through sieve, pressing through as much pumpkin as possible. What remains in sieve should be very dry; discard it.

3 Fill tea kettle with water; bring to a boil. Whisk egg yolks into pumpkin mixture. Pour custard into 6 (1/2-cup) ramekins or custard cups (see below). Place in deep baking dish or roasting pan; set in oven. Carefully pour boiling water into dish or pan until it comes halfway up sides of ramekins. Cover with aluminum foil, crimping it loosely to pan.

4 Bake 25 to 30 minutes or until custard is just set. Cool on wire rack. Serve warm or cover and chill 3 hours before serving.

6 servings.

Preparation time: 35 minutes. Ready to serve: 1 hour, 20 minutes.

Per serving: 225 calories, 14.5 g total fat (7.5 g saturated fat), 245 mg cholesterol, 90 mg sodium, 1.5 g fiber.

PEAR, CRANBERRY AND ORANGE COMPOTE

The longer you leave the pears in the liquid, the more color they absorb from the cranberries. If you can, marinate them overnight — they will look like huge rubies by the time you serve them!

	Juice of 1 lemon
4 to 6	Bartlett, Anjou or Comice pears
3	cups spicy white wine, such as Gewürztraminer or Riesling
1	cup sugar, plus more to taste
2	tablespoons dried orange peel
2	tablespoons grated orange peel
4	cups fresh cranberries, washed
1	cup fresh orange sections, membranes removed

❶ Fill medium bowl half full with water; add lemon juice. Using vegetable peeler or very sharp paring knife, peel pears, leaving stems intact; place each pear in lemon water after peeling.

❷ Pour wine into saucepan large enough to hold pears almost snug. Bring sugar, dried orange peel and grated orange peel to a boil over medium heat. Stir until sugar is dissolved.

❸ Drain pears; carefully place them stem-end up in syrup. Add enough water to cover pears completely. Bring liquid to a boil; reduce heat. Simmer until pears are tender when pierced with bamboo skewer. Using slotted spoon, transfer pears to bowl; set aside.

❹ Increase heat; simmer syrup about 10 minutes or until reduced by ⅓. Stir in cranberries; cook until tender, about 10 minutes. (Be certain all cranberries have popped open.) Remove from heat.

❺ Return pears to cranberry mixture, turning them on their sides to fully submerge. Let rest at room temperature 1 hour or refrigerate up to 2 days. To serve, gently reheat. Set each pear in center of soup plate; fold orange sections into cranberry mixture. Divide mixture among servings.

6 servings.

Preparation time: 35 minutes. Ready to serve: 2 hours, 5 minutes.

Per serving: 300 calories, 1 g total fat (0 g saturated fat), 0 mg cholesterol, 10 mg sodium, 10 g fiber.

LEMON MOUSSE

Voluptuous and as ethereal as a cloud, this tender mousse should please even those without much of a sweet tooth.

½ cup (1 stick) unsalted butter
1 cup sugar
  Dash salt
3 tablespoons grated lemon peel
⅔ cup fresh lemon juice, strained
8 egg yolks
1 cup heavy whipping cream
1 cup *Lemon Curd*, chilled (page 103)

❶ Fill bottom of double boiler half full with water; bring to a boil over medium heat. Reduce heat to low so water simmers slowly.

❷ Set top part of double boiler on top of water; add butter. When melted, stir in sugar, salt, lemon peel and lemon juice. Whisk thoroughly. Whisk in egg yolks. Using wooden spoon, stir mixture until it thickens and coats back of spoon, about 15 minutes. Do not let it heat too quickly. Remove from heat, stirring as it cools to room temperature.

❸ In mixing bowl, whip cream until it forms soft peaks. Using rubber spatula, fold ½ of cream into custard, mixing thoroughly but gently. Gently fold in remaining cream. Divide ½ of mousse among 6 to 8 custard cups or dessert goblets. Put a generous spoonful of curd on each portion of mousse; top with remaining mousse. Cover each serving with plastic wrap; chill at least 3 hours before serving.

8 servings.

Preparation time: 40 minutes. Ready to serve: 4 hours, 20 minutes.

Per serving: 460 calories, 35 g total fat (20 g saturated fat), 360 mg cholesterol, 95 mg sodium, 0 g fiber.

FUDGES & CANDY

by Lisa Golden Schroeder

The process of making fudge and candy is often shrouded in mystery, but the activity is in fact not complicated at all. A few special tools and a little extra attention-to-detail is all it takes to become a skilled confectioner.

Sour Apple Lollipops, page 120

Homemade candies are the ultimate gift, whether formally given or enjoyed in the comfort of your own home. The art of candy making is ancient, dating back to the Crusaders, who brought back sugar from the Holy Land in the early Middle Ages. Before that, honey was the most common household sweetener. A highly prized substance, sugar did not become a widespread culinary ingredient until the early 1600s. The word candy comes from the Arabic word for sugar (qand).

The methods for making candy are not complicated, and the processes of making hard candy, chocolate truffles or fudge, caramels, or chewy taffy or gumdrops, depend on the care you take when handling the ingredients. This chapter only touches on the hundreds of types of candy you can make, and gives you simple methods. Here are some of the basics to get you started. You might even use this information to develop your own homemade confections.

INGREDIENTS

Homemade candies, like all high-quality confections, are only as good as the ingredients that go into them. Here's a run-down of the staples of candy-making.

BUTTER. Salted or unsalted butter can be used in candy; either is preferable in taste to margarine. Use only high-quality stick butter (not in tubs or whipped). Always store butter tightly wrapped, as it can pick up surrounding flavors.

CHOCOLATE. Real chocolate is derived from cocoa beans that grow in large pods on trees close to the equator. It is available in bitter or unsweetened, semisweet, bitter-sweet, milk and white varieties, each containing cocoa butter. The choices for chocolate range from grocery store brands to expensive, imported varieties. For most confections, use bar chocolate, versus baking chips (which have wax added to them so they hold their shape during baking). There is also chocolate candy coating (also known as chocolate compound or summer coating). It does not contain cocoa butter, has a higher melting point than real chocolate, and does not need to be tempered. It doesn't taste as good as real chocolate, but it's much easier to handle in warm weather.

COLORINGS. Pastes, gels, liquids and powdered food colors are available. Special powdered colors work well with chocolate. Use liquid food colors in hard candy and gumdrops.

CREAM. Whipping cream with 32% to 36% butterfat is all that's necessary for making candies, versus heavy cream (which has a higher percentage of butter-fat).

DECORATING SUGARS. A wide assortment of decorating sugars can be found to make candies look especially festive. Look for them where cake decorating supplies are sold. Powdered sugar, and unsweetened and sweetened cocoa powders, are also used to coat or decorate candies, so is edible gold leaf, iridescent glitter and other sparkling decors.

FLAVORINGS. Use pure oils or oil-based flavorings. Pure oils work best with chocolate and hard candies. Oil-based flavorings work well with soft candy fillings. Some alcohol-based flavors (liquid vanilla, almond and other flavor extracts) also work in soft candies. Citrus zests, liqueurs and espresso powder are among the many other kinds of flavorings you can use.

NUTS. Whole and chopped nuts, and nut pastes, are often part of traditional candies. Store nuts in the freezer, and toast them in a 350°F oven for 8 to 10 minutes to bring out their maximum flavor before using.

SUGAR. A wide range of sweeteners are used in candy making. Granulated sugar (sucrose) from sugar cane or beets is the most common form. Brown sugar has molasses added to liquid sucrose during processing. Corn syrup is refined from cornstarch, with water added. Corn syrup adds sweetness and moistness to candies, and interferes with sugar crystallization — thus ensuring smooth candy with no graininess. Honey is a natural sweetener produced by bees. It helps keep candies moist. Maple syrup comes from the boiled-down sap of maple trees, and adds a rustic, unique essence all its own.

TOOLS

Making candy can be the most pleasurable cooking you ever do. But like all kinds of cooking, it can be quite simple or become very involved as your skills increase. Here are the minimum essentials for making just about any kind of candy. From here you can move into fancy molds, truffle dippers, copper sugar pans and chocolate tempering machines!

CANDY MOLDS. If you make lollipops, formed chocolate candies or mold candy mints, you'll need to find special molds. Soft flexible rubber molds are used for soft mints and butters. Use heat-tolerant hard plastic or metal molds for hard candies. Other kinds of food-safe plastic molds are used for chocolate.

CANDY (OR SUGAR) THERMOMETER. A good-quality mercury candy thermometer is probably your most important piece of equipment. A thermometer ensures sugar is cooked to the proper temperature for the kind of candy you want to make.

CHOCOLATE THERMOMETER. Needed for tempering chocolate for dipping and molding, this thermometer's temperature readings are much lower (40°F to 130°F) than for a candy thermometer, in one-degree increments.

LARGE PASTRY BAG AND TIPS. Twelve- or 14-inch pastry bags, made from nylon or soft polyester (so they can be washed), are important for piping out truffle mixtures. Use large 2-inch-high metal pastry tips, each with a plain (about ½-inch) opening. You also want a star tip for decorative piping.

TERMS, TECHNIQUES AND TIPS

Depending on the type of candy you enjoy making, methods and their importance will vary. The two most basic techniques involve melting chocolate and cooking sugar.

MELTING AND TEMPERING CHOCOLATE

- Chocolate melts at a very low temperature, and can burn easily or seize up (solidify into a solid mass when liquid comes in contact with the warm melted chocolate) if handled improperly. For many chocolate candy recipes, chopped chocolate can be gently melted in a double-boiler or in a bowl set over hot water. If making truffles centers (often a ganache), heat cream and pour it onto chopped chocolate in a food processor; process until chocolate is melted and smooth.

- If you plan on dipping candy centers in chocolate (as with truffles) or creating molded chocolate candies that you want to be glossy when solid, then you must temper the chocolate. Tempering is the process that controls the crystalline structure of the cocoa butter molecule, which has several different melting points. Tempering gives chocolate a shiny, unblemished appearance, a smooth texture and a nice snap when broken or bitten into.

- There are a few different methods for tempering chocolate, and some candy makers even have machines that melt and hold chocolate at the right temperature. The basic technique is to heat the chocolate, cool it, then heat it once more. This stabilizes the cocoa butter crystals.

118

COOKED SUGAR KNOW-HOW

- Have an accurate candy thermometer at the ready. To check its accuracy, bring a pan of water to a boil; the thermometer should register 212°F. If the reading is higher or lower, take the difference into account when testing the temperature while making candy. Once you've become more experienced with cooking sugar, you can use the cold water test to determine candy doneness. Test hardness of cooked sugar by dropping a small amount of cooking mixture into a cupful of very cold water. Test the hardness with your fingers.

- Always use the recommended size saucepan called for in a recipe. A smaller or larger pan could affect the cooking time of a sugar syrup.

- To prevent grainy candy, dissolve sugar completely over low heat. Wash down the sides of the pan with a pastry brush dipped in water to dissolve any sugar crystals that could cause a cooked sugar syrup to crystallize. Some recipes call for covering the pan for 2 to 3 minutes once the mixture boils, then uncovering and cooking with the thermometer. Doing this also helps wash down sugar crystals from the sides of the pan.

- Once a sugar syrup begins boiling, do not stir until the desired temperature has been reached. Don't scrape the bottom of the pan when pouring candy out of the pan. Don't stir candy during the cooling period (until directed in a recipe, say for taffy, which gets worked after it's cool enough to handle).

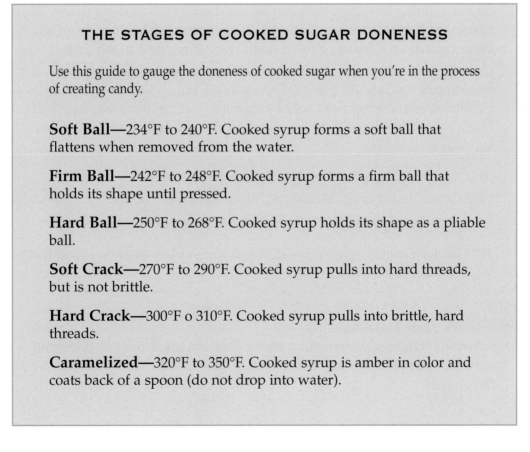

THE STAGES OF COOKED SUGAR DONENESS

Use this guide to gauge the doneness of cooked sugar when you're in the process of creating candy.

Soft Ball—234°F to 240°F. Cooked syrup forms a soft ball that flattens when removed from the water.

Firm Ball—242°F to 248°F. Cooked syrup forms a firm ball that holds its shape until pressed.

Hard Ball—250°F to 268°F. Cooked syrup holds its shape as a pliable ball.

Soft Crack—270°F to 290°F. Cooked syrup pulls into hard threads, but is not brittle.

Hard Crack—300°F o 310°F. Cooked syrup pulls into brittle, hard threads.

Caramelized—320°F to 350°F. Cooked syrup is amber in color and coats back of a spoon (do not drop into water).

SOUR APPLE LOLLIPOPS

These tart and sweet hard suckers grab the heart of the kid in all of us! This candy is also pictured on pages 114-115.

20   hard candy molds or 1 (24-count)
      hard candy ball mold
20   to 24 sucker sticks
 2   cups sugar
¾   cup warm water
½   cup light corn syrup
 1   teaspoon sour apple
      hard candy flavoring
      or oil
 2   drops liquid green food color

❶ Line baking sheet with aluminum foil; spray foil with nonstick cooking spray. Place metal lollipop molds on sheets; insert sticks. Spray molds with cooking spray (or if using candy ball mold, spray inside with cooking spray). Be sure that molds lie very flat.

❷ In 2-quart saucepan*, mix sugar, warm water and corn syrup. Place pan over high heat; bring to a rapid boil, stirring constantly with wooden spoon. Reduce heat to medium. Cover pan; let boil 2 to 3 minutes (this washes down any sugar crystals on sides of pan that could cause graininess in the candy).

❸ Uncover pan; insert candy thermometer. Cook over medium heat until temperature reaches 300°F to 310°F (hard-crack stage). Remove pan from heat. Gently stir sugar syrup until bubbles disappear; stir in flavoring and food color. Using a small metal or candy funnel, carefully pour hot syrup into molds. Cool lollipops completely.

20 (1½-inch) lollipops or 24 (⅝-inch) sour ball suckers.

Preparation time: 1 hour, 15 minutes. Ready to serve: 2 hours.

Per serving: 100 calories, 0 g total fat (0 g saturated fat), 0 mg cholesterol, 10 mg sodium, 0 g fiber.

TIP *To clean cooking pan, fill with warm water; place back on stove. Boil until sugar residue is dissolved.

VARIATION **More Flavorings**
Substitute root beer, watermelon, cherry, butterscotch, lemon or cinnamon-apple flavoring for sour apple flavoring. Change food color as desired to reflect flavor used.

MAPLE ORANGE GUMDROPS

Fruit jelly candies are classic, endearing favorites of the sweets world.

   1 cup sugar
   1 cup maple-flavored syrup
  ¾ cup orange juice
   1 (1¾-oz.) pkg. powdered fruit pectin
1½ teaspoon baking soda
     Granulated maple sugar or colored sugars

① Line 9x5-inch loaf pan with aluminum foil; spray with nonstick cooking spray.

② In 1½-quart saucepan, bring sugar and maple syrup to a boil over medium-high heat, stirring constantly until sugar is dissolved. Insert candy thermometer; cook until temperature registers 280°F (soft-crack stage), without stirring.

③ Meanwhile, in 2-quart saucepan, bring orange juice, pectin and baking soda to a boil, stirring constantly (mixture will be foamy); reduce heat to low. Slowly pour hot sugar mixture in a thin stream into orange juice mixture, stirring constantly. Remove from heat.

④ Let stand 2 minutes; skim foam off top. Pour mixture into pan. Let stand uncovered at room temperature 24 hours. Lift candy from pan with foil; cut into ¾-inch squares with knife dipped in sugar. Roll candies in maple sugar. Let stand uncovered at room temperature 1 hour. Store airtight.

About 72 candies.

Preparation time: 1 hour. Ready to serve: 25 hours.

Per serving: 30 calories, 0 g total fat (0 g saturated fat), 0 mg cholesterol, 10 mg sodium, .5 g fiber.

CINNAMON CAPPUCCINO CARAMELS

These melt-in-your-mouth caramels are rich, creamy and very chewy. Their distinct flavor and color comes from the caramelization of sugar and milk products. Use brown sugar to greatly heighten the flavor of these caramels.

- 2 cups packed light brown sugar
- 2 cups whipping cream
- 3/4 cup light corn syrup
- 1/2 cup (1 stick) unsalted butter
- 1 tablespoon instant-coffee granules
- 1/2 teaspoon ground cinnamon

1. Line 8-inch square pan with aluminum foil; butter foil.

2. In 3-quart saucepan, whisk together brown sugar, cream, corn syrup, butter, instant coffee and cinnamon. Bring to a boil over medium heat, stirring constantly. Insert candy thermometer; cook until temperature registers 248°F (firm-ball stage), stirring frequently.

3. Remove from heat; quickly pour mixture into pan, smoothing top. Cool completely.

4. When candy is firm, remove from pan using the foil. Use buttered knife to cut candy into small pieces; wrap in squares of parchment paper, twisting ends.

About 72 candies.

Preparation time: 45 minutes. Ready to serve: 2 hours, 45 minutes.

Per serving: 65 calories, 3.5 g total fat (2 g saturated fat), 10 mg cholesterol, 10 mg sodium, 0 g fiber.

VARIATION **Mocha Caramels**
Heat 2 oz. chopped unsweetened chocolate with brown sugar mixture. Omit cinnamon.

$\mathcal{P}$EANUT BUTTER FUDGE TRUFFLES

These truffles are pictured on page 124. Look for Mexican vanilla in Latin American markets — its flavor is unique and delicious with the peanut butter filling. Good-quality pure vanilla extract, commonly found in most grocery stores, is probably from Tahiti or Madagascar. See page 118 for the chocolate tempering directions you'll need for dipping candies. This recipe can be easily doubled, especially if you're making the truffles for gifts.

¼	cup (½ stick) unsalted butter
⅓	cup creamy peanut butter
2	teaspoons Mexican or Tahitian vanilla
1½ to 1¾	cups powdered sugar
8	oz. good-quality bittersweet chocolate, finely chopped, melted, tempered

❶ Line baking sheet with parchment paper. In small saucepan heat butter and peanut butter over medium-low heat until melted and smooth. Stir in vanilla and enough powdered sugar to make firm but moist mixture that can be formed. Roll mixture into 1-inch balls. Set aside until ready to dip in chocolate, or sprinkle with cocoa (see photo page 124).

❷ One by one, drop truffle centers into melted chocolate; carefully lift them out with a fork, twisting candies to create a swirl of chocolate on top of each one. Place dipped candies on baking sheet. When all centers are dipped, drizzle with any remaining chocolate. Let truffles set at room temperature or refrigerate them 10 to 15 minutes. When set, place ruffles in paper candy cups. Store airtight up to 1 month in refrigerator or 2 months in freezer.

18 truffles.

Preparation time: 45 minutes. Ready to serve: 1 hour.

Per serving: 155 calories, 10.5 g total fat (5 g saturated fat), 5 mg cholesterol, 25 mg sodium, 1 g fiber.

VARIATION **Cashew Raspberry Truffles**
Substitute cashew butter for peanut butter; stir in 1 tablespoon raspberry liqueur for vanilla in centers. Dip in chocolate as directed. Garnish each truffle with 1 cashew half.

VARIATION **Almond Joy Truffles** (See photo, page 124)
Substitute almond butter for peanut butter and ½ teaspoon coconut extract for vanilla. Dip centers in chocolate as directed; roll in sweetened shredded coconut.

Peanut Butter Fudge Truffle dipped in chocolate, page 123

Almond Joy Truffle, page 123

Peanut Butter Fudge Truffles sprinkled with cocoa, page 123

Hazelnut Cream Fudge, page 123

HAZELNUT CREAM FUDGE

Pictured at left, this traditionally made, soft and creamy fudge is worth the extra effort. By slowly cooking the fudge mixture to the soft-ball stage, cooling it, and then beating to evenly distribute sugar crystals, you are guaranteed a supremely smooth fudge that is far superior to anything store-bought.

1/2 cup (1 stick) unsalted butter
3/4 cup whipping cream
1/2 cup half-and-half
3 1/2 cups sugar
1/8 teaspoon salt
2 tablespoons hazelnut liqueur
1/2 cup toasted and coarsely chopped hazelnuts*

❶ Line 8-inch square pan with aluminum foil; butter foil.

❷ In 3-quart saucepan, melt 1/2 cup butter. Stir in cream, half-and-half, sugar and salt with wooden spoon. Bring mixture to a boil, brushing down sides of pan with wet pastry brush dipped in warm water.

❸ Insert candy thermometer into pan; cook without stirring until it registers 238°F (soft-ball stage). Remove pan from heat. Let mixture cool until it registers 120°F, about 20 minutes or until bottom of pan feels lukewarm. Stir in liqueur; beat with wooden spoon 10 to 15 minutes or until mixture thickens and loses its shine. Beat in hazelnuts until well blended.

❹ Scrape fudge into pan. Use fingertips or off-set spatula to even top and press fudge into corners of pan. Cool on wire rack until completely firm. Remove fudge from pan by lifting it out with the foil. Invert onto cutting board; cut into 1-inch squares. Store fudge between layers of parchment paper in airtight container or tin. Fudge will keep 1 month refrigerated or 10 days at room temperature.

64 (1-inch) pieces.

Preparation time: 1 hour, 30 minutes. Ready to serve: 4 hours, 30 minutes.

Per serving: 75 calories, 3 g total fat (1.5 g saturated fat), 5 mg cholesterol, 5 mg sodium, 0 g fiber.

TIP *To toast hazelnuts, spread on baking sheet; bake at 375°F for about 10 minutes or until lightly browned. Cool.

VARIATION **Gianduja (pronounced john-DO-ya) Cream Fudge**
Drizzle each piece of Hazelnut Cream Fudge with melted milk chocolate; let stand until chocolate is set.

COOKIES 'N CREAM CHUNK FUDGE

Short on time but long on the desire to give the gift of creamy, decadent fudge? Try this no-fail version of a rich dark chocolate confection, studded with chunks of white cookies 'n cream chocolate and flavored with orange liqueur.

- 1 lb. semisweet or bittersweet chocolate, finely chopped
- 1 (14-oz.) can sweetened condensed milk
- 2 teaspoons orange-flavored liqueur
- 18 cookies 'n cream candies (white chocolate candies with chocolate wafer crumbs inside), cut into fourths or 6 oz. white chocolate, cut into chunks

1. Line 8-inch square pan with aluminum foil; butter foil.

2. In large metal bowl placed over saucepan of simmering water, gently melt chocolate. Stir in sweetened condensed milk until smooth.

3. Remove bowl from heat; stir in liqueur. Let cool 3 minutes. Stir in cookies 'n cream candies; spread fudge evenly in pan. Refrigerate 2 hours or until firm.

4. Remove fudge from pan by lifting it out with the foil. Invert onto cutting board; cut into 1-inch squares. Store in refrigerator.

64 (1-inch) pieces.

Preparation time: 45 minutes. Ready to serve: 2 hours, 45 minutes.

Per serving: 70 calories, 3.5 g total fat (2 g saturated fat), 5 mg cholesterol, 10 mg sodium, .5 g fiber.

VARIATION **Almond Marbled Fudge**
Melt 8 oz. chopped chocolate and $1/2$ can (about $1/2$ cup plus 2 tablespoons) sweetened condensed milk together as directed. Remove from heat; stir in $1/2$ teaspoon almond extract. Melt 8 oz. chopped white chocolate and remaining $1/2$ can sweetened condensed milk together; stir in $1/4$ cup toasted chopped almonds. Spoon large dollops of each chocolate mixture randomly into prepared pan. Drag tip of a knife or wooden skewer through fudge, creating marbled effect. Refrigerate until firm. Cut into diamonds.

ST. CATHERINE'S PULLED TAFFY

In the United States, a mention of taffy conjures up visions of chewy boardwalk "saltwater" candies or old-fashioned taffy pulls. But one of the most interesting stories behind taffy comes from France. St. Catherine, a venerated saint from the Middle Ages, became the patron saint of unmarried girls. For centuries (as recently as the mid-1960s), November 25 was celebrated as a holiday honoring young French girls (catherinettes) who were still unmarried at age 25. They would receive gifts and wear silly hats. In French-speaking Québec, Canada, housewives would make tire Sainte-Catherine — or pulled taffy. The molasses-based candy was pulled until it turned light, then was quickly braided to look like tresses and snipped into bite-size pieces. Here it is.

    3   cups sugar
    1   cup each water, light corn syrup
    1   teaspoon salt
    ¼   cup (½ stick) unsalted butter
    2   teaspoons vanilla, almond or rum extract or 1 tablespoon peppermint extract*
        Food color, as desired

1. Butter 15x10x1-inch pan. In 4-quart saucepan, mix sugar and water. Stir in corn syrup and salt. Bring mixture to a boil over medium heat, stirring constantly, washing down sides of pan with pastry brush dipped in warm water. Stir in butter. Insert candy thermometer; cook until temperature registers 256°F (hard-ball stage), without stirring. Remove pan from heat; stir in desired extract and color (you can wait to add color to portions of candy as you pull it, if desired). Pour mixture into pan. Let stand until cool enough to handle.

2. Using buttered hands, pull taffy until satiny, light in color (you're incorporating air into the candy, creating its characteristic chewy texture) and stiff. Place taffy on buttered sheets of parchment paper. Pull into long strips (try your hand at braiding or twisting strands together); cut into 1-inch pieces with scissors sprayed with nonstick cooking spray. Wrap candy in parchment paper squares, twisting ends, or store airtight between layers of parchment paper.

About 60 candies.

Preparation time: 1 hour. Ready to serve: 1 hour, 30 minutes.

Per serving: 60 calories, 1 g total fat (.5 g saturated fat), 5 mg cholesterol, 45 mg sodium, 0 g fiber.

TIP *A few drops of flavor oils can be substituted for liquid extracts — flavor options are greater with flavor oils.

SPICY SESAME NUT CLUSTERS

Here's an addictive batch of sweet-hot candy, sporting a spicy kick and rich flavor. Peppercorns actually have a sweetness to their flavor that enhances nut candies, while a bit of salt balances the ultra-sweetness of caramelized sugar. Follow the cooking times and you can make this without a candy thermometer.

- ¼ cup (½ stick) unsalted butter
- ½ cup sugar
- 2 tablespoons honey
- 1 teaspoon freshly cracked black peppercorns or ¼ teaspoon cayenne pepper
- 3 cups mixed salted nuts
- 2 tablespoons sesame seeds

1. Line large baking sheet with aluminum foil; butter foil.
2. In 2-quart saucepan, heat ¼ cup butter, sugar, honey and peppercorns over medium heat until melted, smooth and bubbly. Cover; cook 1 minute.
3. Stir in nuts and sesame seeds; increase heat to medium-high. Cook uncovered, stirring constantly, about 5 minutes or until nuts are fragrant and lightly browned and syrup is dark golden.
4. Quickly pour mixture onto baking sheet, spreading as thinly as possible. Cool at least 15 minutes or until brittle. Peel candy away from foil; break into pieces.

About 1 lb.

Preparation time: 30 minutes. Ready to serve: 45 minutes.

Per serving: 230 calories, 18.5 g total fat (4 g saturated fat), 5 mg cholesterol, 175 mg sodium, 2.5 g fiber.

VARIATION **Western Spiced Nut Crunch**
Substitute pecan, walnut or macadamia nut halves for mixed nuts, packed light brown sugar for sugar and 1 teaspoon chili powder for cracked peppercorns. Omit sesame seeds.

TAJ MAHAL TRUFFLE CUPS

If you're going to a special event or planning a formal evening, consider making these beautiful candies to treat your guests or give as a hostess gift.

6	oz. dark chocolate-flavored candy coating, chopped (unless in wafer form)
24	tiny paper candy cups
1/3	cup whipping cream
1	cinnamon stick
8	whole cardamom seeds
6	oz. white chocolate, finely chopped
2	tablespoons unsalted butter, softened
1	tablespoon rose water
	Edible gold leaf or gold powder (optional)

❶ In double boiler or metal bowl set over saucepan of simmering water, heat candy coating until melted and smooth. Using small metal spatula, clean paint brush or back of small measuring spoon, spread coating evenly over bottom and up sides of insides of paper candy cups (about 1 teaspoon per cup). Set cups on rimmed baking sheet; set aside until coating hardens.

❷ In small saucepan, heat cream, cinnamon stick and cardamom seeds to just boiling. Remove from heat; let stand 10 minutes. Place white chocolate, butter and rose water in medium metal bowl; set over saucepan of hot water. Return cream to heat; return to just under a boil. Strain cream into white chocolate mixture. Stir with rubber spatula until chocolate is melted and mixture is smooth. Cover; refrigerate 40 to 50 minutes, stirring frequently, or until mixture is thick and mounds when dropped from spoon (this is a ganache*).

❸ Spoon ganache filling into pastry bag with large star tip. Pipe mixture into candy-coated cups. Refrigerate about 30 minutes or until firm. Peel paper from cups. Decorate with flakes of gold leaf, if desired.

24 candies.

Preparation time: 1 hour. Ready to serve: 2 hours.

Per serving: 90 calories, 6 g total fat (4 g saturated fat), 10 mg cholesterol, 10 mg sodium, .5 g fiber.

TIP *Stir 1/4 cup finely ground pistachio nuts into ganache.

LAVENDER WALNUT PRALINES

Wrap pralines in pretty papers and in foils for gift-giving treats (see picture below).

1½	cups packed light brown sugar
1	cup half-and-half
2	tablespoons light corn syrup
2	tablespoons butter
1	tablespoon dark molasses
1½	cups black walnut halves
2	teaspoons dried lavender

❶ Line two baking sheets with aluminum foil; spray foil with nonstick cooking spray. In 3-quart saucepan, bring brown sugar, half-and-half, corn syrup, butter and molasses to a boil over medium heat, stirring to dissolve sugar.

❷ Insert candy thermometer; cook until temperature registers 236°F (soft-ball stage), stirring occasionally. Remove from heat; stir in walnuts and lavender. Let stand 1 minute. Beat with wooden spoon about 3 minutes or until praline mixture cools slightly, thickens and pulls away from sides of pan. Quickly spoon praline mixture by tablespoonfuls onto baking sheets.

❸ Cool 3 hours or until firm. Store, tightly covered, in cool place or refrigerated up to 3 days.

18 candies.

Preparation time: 30 minutes. Ready to serve: 3 hours, 30 minutes.

Per serving: 160 calories, 8 g total fat (2 g saturated fat), 10 mg cholesterol, 25 mg sodium, .5 g fiber.

ICE CREAM & FROZEN DESSERTS

by Mary Evans

Who says dessert has to be be hot, warm ... or even room temperature? Making ice cream and other frozen desserts is surprisingly easy ... and the end results are refreshing and wonderful.

Peach Melba, page 138

There's something special about frozen desserts. We all love the refreshing coolness of frosty cream or fruit based treats. Whether licked from a cone or spooned from a dish, their icy wonder slowly melts in your mouth to deliver bursts of lovely flavor.

Many cultures chill liquids into solid desserts. The origins date back to the 16th or early 17th century, when inventors mixed snow and ice with salt to make a brine with a temperature well below normal freezing. This brine became a bath for base mixtures they froze, producing the first ices. Over the centuries the process continued, with bases shaken, not stirred, in brine baths. This method works better for martinis than ice cream, and smooth-textured results weren't possible until Nancy Johnson, an American, invented a crank freezer with a dasher to churn the base as it froze. She came up with this idea in 1846, and we use the same process to make ice cream today.

INGREDIENTS

Frozen desserts contain many ingredients, some playing a more critical role than others in the resulting texture. Essentially, in making ice creams and ices, ice crystals form but not all of the mixture freezes solidly. The following list highlights the ingredients that play key roles in balancing frozen versus liquid for optimum texture.

MILK. Milk provides a dairy base for frozen desserts and also affects the final consistency. As the water portion freezes, milk solids keep ice crystals small by taking up space while the crystals attempt to grow. Milk, particularly condensed or evaporated milk, also contains lactose, which can produce a sandy texture in finished ice cream. For the best texture, it's important to balance the amount of milk with cream.

HALF-AND-HALF. Because half-and-half, by definition, contains both milk and cream, it contributes both ingredients' qualities to the finished product. Shirley Corriher, noted food scientist, recommends heating milk or half-and-half above 175°F for a better texture.

CREAM. Cream also contributes milk solids but it is the fat content, particularly when using heavy whipping cream, that provides its real contribution to ice cream. Fat traps air when whipped or stirred and keeps ice crystals small by coating them. It also contributes a rich feel to the ice cream when it's in your mouth.

SUGAR. Sugar lowers a liquid's freezing point. In ice creams and ices, sugar dissolves and goes into solution. As the solution chills, some of the water freezes. This gives the resulting syrupy mixture an even higher sugar content, dropping the syrup's freezing point even lower. The process continues as more and more of the ice cream — or any ice mixture — freezes. The remaining syrup, suspended in ice crystals, allows frozen desserts to be scooped. Without it, the desserts would be brick hard. The more sugar a frozen dessert contains, the softer it will be; the less it contains, the harder it will be.

FRUIT. Fruit adds flavor and sugar to ice creams and fruit ices. The sugar content of the fruit is important to remember when deciding how much additional sugar to add to a recipe. In making frozen desserts, fruit with a higher sugar content requires less additional sugar in the base mixture.

WATER. Rather than simply freeze pureed fruit with sugar, add water to fruit ices to clarify the fruit's flavor. Another advantage to water-based sugar syrups is that the sugar is already dissolved when added.

EMULSIFIERS AND OTHER ADDITIONS. Egg yolks are wonderful emulsifiers, contributing a silky feel to the finished ice cream. For food safety reasons, make sure to heat egg yolks above 160°F before using. Instant pudding mixes, low or nonfat dairy products, and preserves containing pectin, all enhance mouth feel and appeal. Lemon juice, salt and extracts enhance flavor.

AIR. Air helps contribute to the final texture of ice cream. Churning traps air, making the mixture less dense. Inexpensive commercial ice creams take this process to an extreme, in some cases doubling the amount of volume through air. This results in an overly fluffy consistency.

TOOLS

There are a variety of ice cream makers available. While they have various advantages in terms of convenience, all produce better results than simply placing a base mixture in the freezer. The stirring, or churning, incorporates air and prevents large ice crystals from forming. For today's lifestyle and the money, the self-contained, electric ice cream makers with metal canisters are the best choice. Because these units eliminate the need for extra ice or salt, they are more convenient than other types. If space allows, simply store the canister in your freezer. Then, making your own ice cream is a breeze. The following types of ice cream makers are available in both hand-cranked (manually) and electric models.

BRINE-BASED: This type of ice cream maker consists of a tub with an inner metal canister and a dasher. The canister rests in the middle of the tub and is surrounded by a brine solution of salt, ice and water. It is important to use the proper proportions. Too much salt lets the mixture in the canister chill too quickly, causing the bottom and sides to freeze solid before being incorporated by the dasher. The dasher is a slotted paddle that aerates the mixture and is cranked manually or electrically. The salt and ice used in these types of makers may be either rock salt and crushed ice, or table salt and ice cubes. Follow directions included at purchase for optimum results.

SELF-CONTAINED: These units generally have a metal canister with insides containing a coolant solution. Place the canister in the freezer for the recommended period of time before using. These models also have an exterior container to hold the canister and an interior dasher to aerate the mixture, again turned manually or electrically. There are also expensive refrigeration types of ice cream makers that are totally self-contained. The machine churns and freezes the base with the flip of a switch, and requires no ice or pre-freezing.

TERMS AND TECHNIQUES

The following terms describe various frozen desserts. Some cover broad classes of desserts and some specify a particular product.

ICE CREAM. Ice cream is a mixture of sweetened, frozen cream and milk. When made with a custard base, it is sometimes referred to as **frozen custard**. The French call ice cream **glacé**, which often has a high proportion of cream. Italians refer to frozen desserts, and particularly ice cream, as **gelato**, which is generally denser than American or French ice cream. When made with yogurt, ice cream becomes **frozen yogurt**.

SEMI-FREDDO. Meaning semi-cold or semi-frozen in Italian, the texture of this frozen dessert is softer and lighter than gelato. It is often served partially thawed.

SORBETS. These smooth ices contain no dairy products. They get their texture from a proper balance of sugar-containing ingredients and water. Fruit-based sorbets that contain some milk or cream are called **sherbets**. **Granitas** are sorbets made without churning, and with less sugar. They have a more crystalline texture. Sorbets and granitas containing fruit are both considered **fruit ices**.

SUNDAE. This term describes a type of ice cream presentation. Consisting of scoops of ice cream topped with sauces or syrups, it's named after Sunday, the day this treat was originally served. Other presentation terms include **bombe**, a molded and layered frozen dessert, and **parfait**, a confection consisting of alternating layers of ice cream and syrups or fruits.

TIPS AND INSIGHTS

Here are some tips and insights to remember when making your ice cream.

- Involve your kids in the process. For the quickest results, choose a recipe that doesn't require pre-cooking. If there are many eager hands available, using a hand-cranked ice cream maker might be fun. Otherwise stick to the electric models. Have bowls available and skip the final ripening. For immediate gratification, spoon the soft ice cream right from the ice cream maker.

- No matter what type of ice cream maker you are using, follow the manufacturer's directions for optimum results. Companies spend many hours testing their product for the best outcome, and pass their tips on to you in their instruction booklets.

- If the recipe calls for "aging" pre-cooked mixtures in the refrigerator, do so for at least 4 hours to get the best texture in the finished product. This ensures that many small ice crystals form in the ice cream maker, rather than fewer large ones. If time allows, refrigerate overnight for even better flavor.

- To reduce fat, you can add more milk and less cream, but remember that the texture will be affected accordingly.

- If adding chunks of fruit to ice cream, add them toward the end of the freezing process and serve the ice cream fairly quickly. Otherwise these chunks of fruit become extremely hard and difficult to eat. Soaking chunks of fruit in alcohol, or allowing the fruit to macerate in sugar, helps remedy this situation by lowering the freezing point of the fruit.

- When creating your own fruit-based sorbets, try using some preserves as well as fruit. Preserves enhance mouth feel and intensify flavor. Remember that they add a great deal of sweetness as well, so reduce the sugar called for by 1 tablespoon for every tablespoon of preserves.

- Don't try to keep homemade ice cream too long. Since self-defrosting home freezers cycle on and off, ice cream melts slightly and re-freezes, allowing larger ice crystals to form and affect quality.

PEACH MELBA

This ice cream is pictured on pages 132-133. Peach Melba gets its name from 19th century opera singer Nellie Melba. This version adds baked meringues for extra crunch and texture.

VANILLA ICE CREAM
1½ cups milk
1 cup heavy cream
4 egg yolks
½ cup sugar
1 teaspoon vanilla

MERINGUE SHELLS
2 egg whites
¼ teaspoon cream of tartar
6 tablespoons sugar
2 tablespoons powdered sugar

RASPBERRY SAUCE
1½ cups raspberries, fresh or frozen and thawed
½ cup raspberry jam
1 tablespoon Kirsch or orange juice

PEACHES
6 peach halves, canned in juice, drained
6 tablespoons Kirsch (optional)

❶ In medium saucepan, heat milk and ½ cup of the cream over medium heat until scalded.

❷ Meanwhile, in medium bowl, whisk together egg yolks and ½ cup sugar. Slowly whisk ¾ cup of scalded milk mixture into yolks; whisk back into pan. Cook, stirring constantly over medium heat, until mixture thickens slightly and coats back of spoon. Immediately pour into clean bowl; stir in vanilla. Refrigerate, covered, about 4 hours to age. Whip remaining ½ cup cream to soft peaks; fold into chilled custard. Freeze in ice cream maker according to manufacturer's directions. Remove to chilled container; cover. Freeze 4 to 5 hours to ripen and firm.

❸ Meanwhile, heat oven to 200°F. Line baking sheet with parchment paper. In medium bowl, beat egg whites at high speed until frothy; beat in cream of tartar. Continue beating to almost stiff peaks; beat in 2 tablespoons of the sugar and powdered sugar. Beat until stiff peaks form. Sprinkle with remaining 4 tablespoons sugar; fold into whites. Immediately spoon whites into 6 mounds on baking sheet. Using back of spoon, flatten slightly and form hollow in center. Bake 2 hours; turn off heat. Let cool in oven 30 minutes. Remove.

❹ To make sauce: In blender or food processor, puree raspberries, jam and 1 tablespoon Kirsch. Strain to remove seeds. If desired, in medium bowl toss peach halves with 6 tablespoons Kirsch; marinate about 30 minutes. To serve, place 1 peach half, hollow-side up, in center of each meringue; add scoop of ice cream. Top with raspberry sauce.

6 servings.

Preparation time: 1 hour, 30 minutes. Ready to serve: 9 hours.

Per serving: 445 calories, 17 g total fat (9.5 g saturated fat), 190 mg cholesterol, 80 mg sodium, 2 g fiber.

TARTUFO NOIR SEMI-FREDDO (CHOCOLATE TRUFFLE SEMI-FREDDO)

This incredibly rich dessert's namesake is the true Tartufo Noir, *or black truffle, dug from the ground in the Italian countryside and used in savory dishes. Here, the dusting of cocoa is reminiscent of the earth that clings to the real truffle.*

1   cup half-and-half
2   eggs, separated
2   tablespoons plus ½ cup sugar
8   oz. semisweet chocolate, chopped
¼   cup water
2   tablespoons unsweetened cocoa

❶ In small saucepan, heat half-and-half over medium heat until scalded.

❷ Meanwhile, in medium bowl, whisk together 2 egg yolks and 2 tablespoons of the sugar. Slowly whisk in about ⅓ of scalded half-and-half; whisk back into pan. Cook, stirring constantly, until mixture thickens slightly and coats back of spoon. Pour into clean metal bowl. Stir in chocolate until melted and smooth. Cool to room temperature.

❸ In medium bowl, beat egg whites until foamy and soft peaks just begin to form; set aside. In small saucepan, heat remaining ½ cup sugar and water over medium-high heat, stirring constantly, until sugar dissolves and mixture comes to a boil. Continue cooking; do not stir. Wash down any sugar granules on sides of pan with pastry brush dipped in cold water. Continue cooking to 248°F (firm-ball stage). Immediately beat egg whites at high speed until almost stiff. Reduce speed to low; slowly beat in sugar syrup. Continue beating at high speed until mixture is room temperature.

❹ Stir ⅓ of egg whites into cooled chocolate mixture with whisk; gently stir in next ⅓ and then final ⅓. Cover; freeze 4 hours or overnight to firm and ripen. When ready to serve, scoop ball of mixture with ice cream scoop onto plate; dust lightly with cocoa. Let rest about 10 minutes before serving.

8 servings.

Preparation time: 1 hour. Ready to serve: 5 hours.

Per serving: 260 calories, 13.5 g total fat (7.5 g saturated fat), 65 mg cholesterol, 30 mg sodium, 2 g fiber.

$\mathcal{B}$LUEBERRY BAKED ALASKA

In this recipe, regular egg whites cannot be heated enough to eliminate potential food safety problems, so use dried egg white powder for the meringue. Dried egg white powder is pasteurized and completely safe. It takes longer to beat though, so keep that in mind.

BLUEBERRY SAUCE
- 2 (16-oz.) pkg. frozen blueberries, thawed
- 1 cup sugar
- ½ cup crème de cassis or orange juice
- ¼ cup lemon juice

BLUEBERRY ICE CREAM
- 2 cups half-and-half
- 4 egg yolks
- ½ cup sugar
- Dash salt
- Reserved blueberry sauce

SPONGE CAKE
- 4 eggs, separated
- ¾ cup plus 2 tablespoons sugar
- ½ teaspoon vanilla
- 1 teaspoon grated lemon peel
- Dash salt
- ¾ cup all-purpose flour

MERINGUE
- 2 tablespoons dried egg white powder
- 6 tablespoons water
- ¼ teaspoon cream of tartar
- Dash salt
- ½ cup plus 1 tablespoon sugar

1 In food processor, process blueberries, 1 cup sugar, crème de cassis and lemon juice to combine. Strain, keeping half for sauce; reserve half for ice cream.

2 In medium saucepan, heat half-and-half over medium heat until scalded. In medium bowl, whisk 4 egg yolks with ½ cup sugar and dash salt. Slowly whisk in ¾ cup of scalded half-and-half; whisk back into pan. Cook, stirring constantly, until mixture thickens and coats back of spoon. Do not boil. Immediately pour into clean bowl; stir in reserved blueberry sauce. Refrigerate, covered, 4 hours to age. Process in ice cream freezer according to manufacturer's directions. Remove to chilled container; store in freezer, covered, while preparing and cooling cake layer.

③ Heat oven to 350°F. Butter and flour two 8-inch square pans. In large mixing bowl, combine 4 egg yolks and ¾ cup of the sugar; beat at medium speed about 3 to 4 minutes or until pale and mixture forms a ribbon when beater is lifted from yolks. Stir in vanilla and lemon peel. In large mixing bowl, beat egg whites and dash salt at medium-high speed until soft peaks form. Add remaining 2 tablespoons sugar; beat at high speed 15 to 20 seconds or until glossy. Fold ¼ of egg whites into yolk mixture to lighten. Sift ¼ cup of the flour over mixture; fold in. Repeat, folding in egg whites and flour alternately. Pour batter into pans. Bake about 15 minutes or just until cake begins to pull away from sides of pan. Allow cake to cool 10 minutes before unmolding. Cool completely. (Freeze remaining cake for later use.)

④ To assemble, cut one 8-inch cake in half, then in half horizontally. Line 8x4-inch loaf pan with plastic wrap. Place 1 cake strip on bottom; top with ⅓ of ice cream. Repeat with layers of cake and ice cream; top with remaining cake strip. Freeze 4 to 5 hours or overnight to harden.

⑤ When ready to serve, heat oven to 500°F. In mixing bowl, beat egg white powder and water at low speed until dissolved. Increase speed to medium-high; beat in cream of tartar and dash salt. Continue beating until soft peaks form. Sprinkle with ½ cup plus 1 tablespoon sugar; beat until stiff and glossy.

⑥ Line baking sheet with parchment paper. Unmold frozen ice cream cake, removing plastic wrap. Cover cake completely with meringue. Bake on baking sheet about 4 minutes or until well browned. Remove to platter; serve immediately. Slice into 8 equal portions. Accompany with blueberry sauce.

8 servings.

Preparation time: 2 hours. Ready to serve: 11 hours.

Per serving: 480 calories, 11.5 g total fat (5.5 g saturated fat), 180 mg cholesterol, 160 mg sodium, 2 g fiber.

$\mathcal{M}$ANGO-GINGER SORBET

When ripe, mangoes yield lightly to pressure. Avoid overly ripe mangoes, which can be fibrous and discolored when peeled.

- 1 cup sugar
- 1½ cups water
- 2 teaspoons grated fresh ginger*
- 2 cups pureed fresh mango pulp (about 2 ripe mangoes weighing about 1¾ lb. total)**
- 1 tablespoon lemon juice

1. In medium saucepan, combine sugar, ½ cup of the water and ginger. Stir over medium heat until sugar dissolves and mixture come to a boil. Boil without stirring 1 minute. Remove from heat; let cool to room temperature.

2. Stir in remaining 1 cup water, pureed mango and lemon juice. Freeze in ice cream maker according to manufacturer's directions. Remove to chilled container; cover. Freeze 4 to 5 hours or overnight to firm and ripen.

10 servings.

Preparation time: 30 minutes. Ready to serve: 6 hours.

Per serving: 100 calories, 0 g total fat (0 g saturated fat), 0 mg cholesterol, 1 mg sodium, .5 g fiber.

TIP *Use a fine grater to grate ginger. While grating, cut off fibers as they appear on the knob of ginger. Make sure to use resulting juices along with the finely grated flesh.

TIP **To puree, peel mangoes. Slice flesh from flat inner seed; pulse in food processor.

PEARS FOSTER

Make this recipe in the fall when pears are at their peak.

3 large, firm ripe pears, cored, cut into eighths
1 tablespoon lemon juice
⅓ cup unsalted butter
¼ cup dark rum
¼ cup packed dark brown sugar
1 tablespoon pear brandy (optional)
1 recipe *Vanilla Ice Cream* (page 138) or 1 recipe *Mascarpone Ice Cream* (page 146) or 3 cups purchased vanilla ice cream

❶ In medium bowl, toss pears with lemon juice.

❷ In large skillet, melt butter over medium-high heat. Add pears; cook in single layer, turning once, 6 to 8 minutes or until just beginning to soften. Remove. Add rum and brown sugar to skillet; cook 5 minutes or until mixture has thickened. Stir in brandy, if desired. Add pears; stir to coat. Serve over ice cream in individual serving bowls.

6 servings.

Preparation time: 15 minutes. Ready to serve: 30 minutes.

Per serving: 470 calories, 27.5 g total fat (15.5 g saturated fat), 215 mg cholesterol, 55 mg sodium, 3 g fiber.

WHITE CHOCOLATE-HAZELNUT GELATO

Look for hazelnut syrup in the coffee section of your grocery store. This type of syrup is often used to make flavored coffees.

2   cups milk
1   cup heavy whipping cream
4   egg yolks
⅓   cup sugar
    Dash salt
4   oz. chopped white chocolate
⅓   cup hazelnut syrup
¼   teaspoon almond extract

❶ In medium saucepan, heat milk and cream over medium heat until scalded.

❷ Meanwhile, in medium bowl, whisk together egg yolks, sugar and salt. Slowly whisk 1 cup of scalded milk mixture into egg mixture; whisk back into remaining milk mixture in saucepan. Continue cooking, stirring constantly, until mixture thickens slightly and coats back of spoon. Immediately pour into clean bowl. Stir in white chocolate until incorporated; stir in hazelnut syrup and almond extract.

❸ Refrigerate, covered, about 4 hours to age. Process in ice cream maker according to manufacturer's directions. Serve immediately in individual bowls or remove mixture to chilled container. Freeze 2 hours to ripen but remain slightly soft.

8 servings.

Preparation time: 30 minutes. Ready to serve: 6 hours, 30 minutes.

Per serving: 280 calories, 17 g total fat (10 g saturated fat), 150 mg cholesterol, 90 mg sodium, 0 g fiber.

HOMEMADE MASCARPONE ICE CREAM WITH AMARETTO-PLUM SAUCE

Mascarpone is a soft, cream-based cheese from Italy. It is much richer and softer than our regular domestic cream cheese.

MASCARPONE ICE CREAM
2   cups half-and-half
1   (8-oz.) carton mascarpone
1/2   vanilla bean, split lengthwise
5   egg yolks
2/3   cup sugar

AMARETTO-PLUM SAUCE
3   firm-ripe plums, pitted, sliced
1   (10-oz.) jar plum jam
1/4   cup almond-flavored liqueur (or 1/4 cup water and 3/4 teaspoon almond extract)

❶ In medium bowl, whisk 1/4 cup of the half-and-half into mascarpone to soften; set aside. Place remaining 1 3/4 cups half-and-half in medium saucepan. Scrape seeds from vanilla bean into half-and-half; add pods. Heat over medium heat until scalded; remove from heat. Allow to steep 10 minutes. Remove pods.

❷ Meanwhile, in medium bowl, whisk together egg yolks and sugar. Whisk 1/2 of scalded cream slowly into egg yolks; whisk back into pan. Cook, stirring constantly, over medium heat until mixture thickens slightly and coats back of spoon. Do not boil. Immediately pour into clean bowl. Cool to room temperature; whisk into mascarpone mixture. Freeze in ice cream maker according to manufacturer's directions. Remove to chilled container; cover and freeze 4 to 5 hours or overnight to firm and ripen.

❸ Before serving, place plums, jam and liqueur in medium saucepan. Melt jam over medium-low heat, stirring often to combine and prevent scorching. When melted, reduce heat to low; continue cooking 5 minutes, stirring occasionally to soften plums slightly. Remove from heat; let cool slightly. Scoop ice cream into individual serving bowls. Spoon Amaretto-Plum Sauce over.

About 4 cups ice cream or 6 to 8 servings.

Preparation time: 30 minutes. Ready to serve: 6 hours.

Per serving: 400 calories, 20.5 g total fat (11.5 g saturated fat), 185 mg cholesterol, 125 mg sodium, .5 g fiber.

BLACK FOREST SUNDAES

While not as creamy as ice cream made in an ice cream maker, this recipe works well for cooks who don't have one. The pudding lends a smoother texture to the finished product.

CHERRY ICE CREAM
- 1 (3.4-oz.) pkg. instant vanilla pudding
- 2 tablespoons sugar
- 1½ cups whipping cream
- ½ teaspoon almond extract
- 1 (16-oz.) pkg. frozen pitted cherries

HOT FUDGE TOPPING
- ⅔ cup sugar
- ¼ cup unsweetened cocoa
- 1 tablespoon cornstarch
- ¼ teaspoon salt
- ¾ cup light corn syrup
- 1 cup whipping cream
- 1 (1-oz.) square unsweetened chocolate, chopped
- 1 tablespoon butter
- 1 tablespoon vanilla

❶ In food processor, pulse instant pudding and 2 tablespoons sugar several times to combine. Add 1½ cups cream and almond extract; process until combined and beginning to thicken. With motor still running, add cherries a handful at a time, reserving 8 cherries for garnish. When all cherries have been incorporated, remove mixture to chilled container. Cover; freeze 4 to 5 hours to firm and ripen.

❷ Meanwhile, in large saucepan, whisk together ⅔ cup sugar, cocoa, cornstarch and salt. Whisk in corn syrup and 1 cup cream. Bring to a boil over medium heat, stirring frequently. Boil 5 minutes, stirring occasionally.

❸ Remove from heat, stir in chocolate, butter and vanilla until incorporated and smooth. Let cool to lukewarm. Spoon over scoops of ice cream in 8 sundae dishes; top each with reserved cherries. Refrigerate any extra sauce, covered, for future use.

8 servings.

Preparation time: 45 minutes. Ready to serve: 4 hours, 45 minutes.

Per serving: 515 calories, 27.5 g total fat (17 g saturated fat), 85 mg cholesterol, 320 mg sodium, 3 g fiber.

MOCHA IRISH CREAM PIE

Make sure to use a dense, premium ice cream when making this pie.

CRUST
   1   cup chocolate cookie crumbs
   ¼   cup sugar
   ¼   cup (½ stick) unsalted butter, melted, cooled

FILLING
   1   pint premium chocolate ice cream
   1   pint premium coffee ice cream
   ⅓   cup Irish Cream liqueur (or ½ cup liquid, non-dairy Irish Crème coffee flavor)
   1   cup lightly sweetened whipped cream
   8   chocolate-covered coffee beans

1. In medium bowl, stir together crumbs and sugar. Add butter; stir to mix well. Press crumb mixture into bottom and up sides of 9-inch pie plate.

2. Scoop chocolate and coffee ice creams into large mixing bowl; let soften about 10 minutes. Add liqueur; stir until well blended. Spoon into crust. Freeze 8 hours or overnight.

3. Remove from freezer 10 minutes before serving. Cut into 8 wedges. Place dollop of whipped cream on each portion; top with chocolate covered coffee beans.

8 servings.

Preparation time: 30 minutes. Ready to serve: 8 hours, 30 minutes.

Per serving: 515 calories, 33 g total fat (17.5 g saturated fat), 100 mg cholesterol, 150 mg sodium, 2.5 g fiber.

PASTRIES & TARTS

by Carole Brown

Light. Elegant. Fruity. Sweet. Heavenly. So many words to describe pastries and tarts ... and so many ways to create some of your tastiest and classiest desserts ever. Here are the secrets behind great pastry and great tarts — and plenty of recipes too.

Individual Apple Tarts, page 159

"Tarts and pastry"— the very words promise something fun and festive. These recipes are ideal for special occasions, but many of them also work well for casual entertaining and occasional family desserts. In addition to several tempting tarts, there are two versatile, light-as-air pastry recipes, Quick Puff Pastry (page 156) *and* Cream Puff Pastry (page 157) *that stand on their own and also serve as the basis for other recipes.*

Quick Puff Pastry is the basis of many elegant creations offered in haute cuisine *restaurants and pastry shop windows — Napoleons, patty shells, wrap for Beef Wellington, cheese straws, turnovers and more. But what transforms ordinary butter and dough into the irresistible melt-in-your-mouth flaky pastry? Folds, folds and more folds! Repeated rolls and folds build up hundreds of layers of butter and dough that rise beautifully in the heat of the oven. That's why the French call it* millefeuille *(thousand-leaf pastry). The shortcut version in this chapter is ideal for the home baker.*

Cream Puff Pastry is another basic of the pastry kitchen, and one that is easily mastered by the home cook. It can transform into éclairs, cream puffs, filled specialty cakes, cheese puffs, a towering croquembouche *(pyramid of cream puffs popular at French weddings), deep-fried* beignets *(fritter), or even miniature puffs to float in consommé.*

Tarts, with their shallow straight sides, are often made from an all-butter dough which is flaky and rather sturdy. Although many people think tarts must be trickier than pies, all-butter dough is quite firm and a little easier to handle than dough made with shortening.

INGREDIENTS

The key to tart success is the cold temperature of water, butter and your hands! Warmth is the enemy.

BUTTER. Although you can make successful pastry with salted butter, I recommend using unsalted butter because of its fresh, clean taste.

CREAM. Heavy whipping cream, with a butterfat content of 36% or more, will give you richer and silkier results, but these recipes can be made with regular whipping cream (30% to 36% butterfat). If you can find it, I prefer cream that has not been ultra-pasteurized.

EGGS. These recipes were created using large eggs.

FLOUR. Pastries are sometimes made with special cake or bread flours. For the sake of simplicity and convenience, all of the recipes in this chapter use all-purpose flour.

MAPLE SYRUP. Choose real maple syrup for baking, not a maple-flavored syrup. Grade B maple syrup, harvested a little later in the sap season than Grade A, is slightly darker and has a more intense flavor.

TOOLS

Here are the basic tools you need for everyday tarts ... and beyond.

1- or 2-inch natural bristle pastry brush. The soft bristles are much kinder to dough than the stiff plastic bristles of inexpensive brushes. Save your natural bristle brush just for pastries.

6- to 8-inch offset icing spatula. This can be used in lieu of a pastry scraper to release dough from the countertop.

12- or 14-inch pastry bag with ½-inch plain tip. Small pastry bags are fine for some jobs, but select one that is at least 12 inches for piping Cream Puff Pastry. You won't have to stop and refill the bag.

Aluminum or porcelain pie weights. If you can't find pie weights, substitute 1 to 2 cups of dried beans such as chick peas — they can be used and reused many times.

Aluminum or tinned-steel tart pans with fluted edges and removable bottoms. These come in many sizes (starting with 4-inch miniature tartlet pans) and shapes (rounds, rectangles and squares). The most useful for home cooking are 8-, 9- and 10-inch rounds. When your tart has cooled, set the pan on a large can and let the outside edge fall away.

Nonstick silicone Silpat sheets or parchment paper. A tool not only for baking, but for cleanup as well.

Pastry blender. This old standby cuts butter into flour.

Pastry (or pizza) cutting wheel. Large or small, these work well for cutting dough, especially puff pastry.

Pastry (board) scraper. Use this tool to toss and cut doughs, and to release them from the countertop.

Rectangular cooling racks. Use this tool to cool your pastries and tarts.

Rolling pin. Depending on what's most comfortable for you, this can be a pin with ball bearings and handles, or a no-handle French-style pin.

When it comes to creating pastries and tarts, it's important to know and understand the basic terms and techniques.

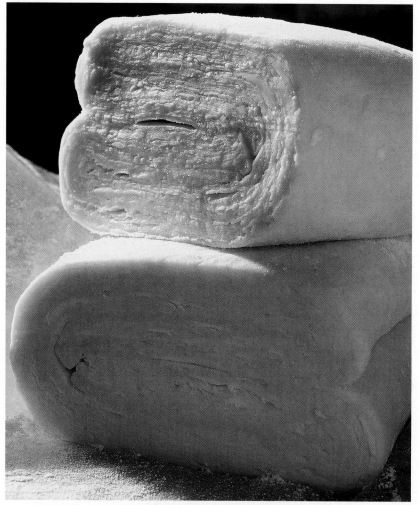

FOLDING OR TURNING. This is the puff pastry technique for enclosing butter in the dough, building up the layers that rise and flake in the heat of the oven. The dough is rolled out and folded (or "turned"), sometimes in thirds like a business letter (a "three-way fold" or "three-fold turn") or in fourths (a "four-way fold" or "four-fold turn").

GLAZING. For a crisp finished tart, try glazing the partly baked tart shell with a light coating of beaten egg or egg white.

LE FRAISAGE. The final step in making tart dough, this is an easy French technique that smooths the dough without kneading or overworking it. On the countertop, smear the dough away from you with several strokes of the heel of your hand. The bits of butter are smeared into small discs, which contribute to the crust's flakiness.

TO BAKE BLIND. This is the process of baking a tart shell with no filling. Sometimes a tart shell is half-baked before filling, to crisp the bottom crust and prevent it from getting soggy. A tart shell can also be completely baked in advance but the filling never baked. Before baking blind, the dough is usually docked (see definition below), covered with parchment paper or aluminum foil and filled with metal or porcelain pie weights (or dried beans) to discourage the pastry from bubbling.

TO DOCK. To prick pastry all over with the tines of a fork (or a special rolling utensil called a docker). This allows steam to escape during baking and discourages pastry dough from bubbling unevenly as it bakes.

TIPS AND INSIGHTS

Follow these tips and you'll always be in pastry heaven!

MIXING THE DOUGH

- Cold ingredients will give you an advantage when making tart dough. Have the butter well-chilled or even partially frozen.

- Before you prepare other ingredients, fill a cup with cold water and drop in one or two ice cubes. When you later measure out the water you need, it will be icy cold.

- Use cutting and sheeting techniques rather than twisting and kneading movements to incorporate the butter into the flour. The goal is thin discs of butter surrounded by dough; as the discs melt in the oven, steam forms and creates flaky layers.

- With experience, you will learn to avoid over mixing the dough. Too much mixing develops gluten; this creates an elastic dough that will snap back as you roll it and shrink when it bakes. If you find the dough is too elastic, let it relax in the refrigerator.

- The food processor can be an excellent tool for making tart dough, but use its power sparingly by pulsing rather than running the machine steadily.

- Chill the dough after mixing for at least 15 minutes; it will be easier to roll out.

- An excellent way to finish and blend the dough is a French technique called *le fraisage* (see page 154).

- If wrapped well to keep out odors, tart dough can be frozen for at least two months.

QUICK PUFF PASTRY TIPS

- If you have any trouble with soft and sticky dough, return it to the refrigerator to chill.

- Use a soft pastry brush to remove excess flour from the dough, especially when you are making the folds.

CREAM PUFF PASTRY TIP

- Once baked, *Cream Puff Pastry* is best filled and served within 1 to 2 hours. You can hold them longer, but they may lose their crispness. If so, refresh them in a 375°F oven for 5 minutes. Baked puffs freeze well. Thaw and re-crisp them in the same way. Once cooked on top of the stove, the pastry doesn't hold well; it should be formed and baked as soon as it is made.

QUICK PUFF PASTRY

Quick Puff Pastry *is a basic of the pastry kitchen. The following recipe makes enough dough to use in two desserts. Make the full recipe, even if you want only half. It's easier to handle the larger amount, and you can freeze what you don't use. Wrapped well, it keeps in the freezer at least two months.*

> 3 cups all-purpose flour
> 1 teaspoon salt
> 1½ cups (3 sticks) cold unsalted butter, cut into ¼-inch cubes
> 1 cup ice water

❶ Using an electric mixer: In large bowl of electric mixer with whisk attachment, stir together flour and salt; add butter. Pour in ice water while mixing. Stop mixing when dough is still very rough and crumbly and butter is in large visible chunks. Put dough on floured surface. Making by hand: In large mixing bowl, mix flour and salt. Add butter; toss to coat with flour. Add ice water; mix with hands or large spatula until dough just barely holds together and butter is still in large visible chunks. Put dough on floured surface.

❷ Smear and press dough into rough rectangle. Keeping counter and rolling pin well-floured, roll dough into 9x12-inch rectangle. Using pastry scraper or icing spatula, lift one end of rectangle and fold into center like a business letter. Lift opposite end and fold on top. (This is called a three-way fold.) This will feel awkward because pastry is rough, but it becomes smooth with subsequent rollings. Cover dough with plastic wrap; refrigerate at least 30 minutes.

❸ Four four-way folds: Roll chilled dough into rectangle that runs north to south. Brush away any excess flour. To make first four-way fold, fold both ends of rectangle into center; straighten edges and corners. Fold in half to make 4 layers. Make a quarter turn with dough so open edge is to your right (the pastry will look like a book that you are about to open). Roll dough again into rectangle that runs north-south; repeat four-way fold. Rewrap dough; let rest in refrigerator at least 30 minutes. Make 2 more four-way folds.

❹ After another rest in refrigerator, dough will be ready to use. If you wish, dough can rest overnight.

About 2 lb. dough, enough for 2 recipes.

Preparation time: 21 minutes. Ready to serve: 2 hours.

Per serving: 120 calories, 9 g total fat (5 g saturated fat), 25 mg cholesterol, 75 mg sodium, 0 g fiber

CREAM PUFF PASTRY

Cream Puff Pastry *is another basic of the pastry kitchen, and one that is easily mastered by the home cook.*

> 1 cup water
> ¼ cup (½ stick) butter
> 1 cup all-purpose flour
> 2 to 3 large eggs

❶ Heat oven to 425°F.

❷ In small saucepan, bring water and butter to a boil. Remove from heat; add flour all at once. Stir with wooden spoon until flour is absorbed and dough forms a ball. Stir over very low heat 1 to 2 minutes until dough is dry and smooth. Remove from heat.

❸ If a film has formed on bottom of pan, transfer dough to clean bowl. Stir in 1 of the eggs by hand or with electric mixer until egg is well-incorporated and dough is smooth. Repeat with second egg. Mix third egg in small bowl; add a little at a time until dough is consistency of soft cookie dough — stiff enough to hold soft peaks but soft enough to pipe easily through a pastry bag. Due to variations in flour and eggs, you may need all or none of third egg.

❹ Shape and bake pastry according to recipe.

About 20 (2-inch) cream puffs.

Preparation time: 20 minutes. Ready to serve: 1 hour, 50 minutes.

Per serving: 50 calories, 3 g total fat (1.5 g saturated fat), 30 mg cholesterol, 20 mg sodium, 0 g fiber.

TIP *It's usually unnecessary to grease baking pans. Puff pastry contains plenty of butter.

.

VANILLA PASTRY CREAM

Because pastry cream is usually used cold, it's easy to make a day ahead and store in the refrigerator. Pastry cream cream is another essential "base" recipe you'll need.

1   cup whole milk
3   egg yolks
⅓   cup plus 1 tablespoon sugar
3   tablespoons all-purpose flour
1   teaspoon vanilla

❶ In saucepan, bring milk to a simmer.

❷ In bowl, blend yolks and ⅓ cup of the sugar. Beat by hand or with electric mixer until mixture is lighter in color. Mix flour and remaining 1 tablespoon of sugar; stir into yolks. Stir ¼ of the hot milk into yolk mixture. Stir while adding remaining milk in a slow stream to prevent eggs from cooking.

❸ Pour pastry cream into clean saucepan (or rinse out milk pan and reuse); place over low heat. Stir until sauce thickens and holds whisk streaks for several moments. Heat to 160°F or higher on an instant-read thermometer. Remove from heat; stir in vanilla.

❹ Cool pastry cream, stirring occasionally to prevent a skin from forming. Place plastic wrap directly on top of pastry cream; refrigerate. Store in refrigerator 4 to 5 days.

About 1½ cups pastry cream.

Preparation time: 15 minutes. Ready to serve: 1 hour, 30 minutes.

Per serving: 120 calories, 4 g total fat (2 g saturated fat), 110 mg cholesterol, 25 mg sodium, 0 g fiber.

VARIATION **Ginger Pastry Cream**
Before cooking pastry cream, steep milk by putting it in saucepan with 8 to 10 thin slices fresh ginger (skin-on is okay); bring to a simmer. Remove from heat; set aside 10 minutes. Strain ginger from milk; proceed with recipe. Decrease vanilla to ¼ teaspoon.

INDIVIDUAL APPLE TARTS

These free-form tarts, pictured on pages 150-151, are also ideal for casual snacks.

CINNAMON TART DOUGH

2	cups all-purpose flour
1/4	cup sugar
1 1/2	teaspoons ground cinnamon
1/2	teaspoon salt
3/4	cup (1 1/2 sticks) cold unsalted butter, cut into 1/2-inch cubes
5 to 6	tablespoons ice water

FILLING

1/4	cup sugar
1/4	cup packed brown sugar
1	teaspoon freshly grated nutmeg
2 to 3	baking apples
1	egg, beaten
	Powdered sugar for garnish (optional)

1 In food processor, pulse flour, 1/4 cup sugar, cinnamon and salt to blend well. Add butter; pulse 15 to 20 times until butter pieces are about half their original size. Add ice water, 1 to 2 tablespoons at a time, through feed tube. Run machine only when pouring water through tube; stop machine while you refill measuring spoon with water. Stop while pastry still looks crumbly and dry, before it comes together in a ball. With spoon, scoop some dough out of bowl; press in your hand. If it holds together well and feels moist, you have probably added enough water. If it seems dry and crumbly, sprinkle on more water 1 tablespoon at a time; pulse briefly to incorporate. Turn dough out onto lightly floured surface.

2 Finish by smearing dough away from you in several strokes with heel of your hand. Fold dough into a ball. It will still be a bit rough in texture and bits of butter will be visible. Wrap in plastic wrap; let rest in refrigerator 30 to 60 minutes. Roll out dough into 12-inch circle (1/2 at a time if you prefer); cut out as many 5 1/2- to 6-inch circles as you can. You should get at least 6; re-rolling scraps will give you at least 2 more. Stack circles separated with parchment paper; reserve in refrigerator.

3 Heat oven to 375°F. In bowl, mix 1/4 cup sugar, brown sugar and nutmeg. Core and cut apples into 12 slices each. Toss slices in sugar mixture. Put 3 to 4 apple slices in center of each chilled pastry round. Dip your fingers in beaten egg to use as "glue"; turn up edge of each circle to partially enclose apples. Pleat edges by pinching dough in several places as you work around tartlet. If any juice remains in apple bowl, drizzle it into tarts. Brush more egg wash on tops and sides of tartlets with pastry brush or your fingers. Bake 30 to 40 minutes or until apples are cooked and tartlets are browned and bubbly. Cool on wire racks. Serve warm or at room temperature. Dust tarts with powdered sugar, if desired.

8 servings.

Preparation time: 20 minutes. Ready to serve: 2 hours.

Per serving: 370 calories, 18.5 g total fat (11 g saturated fat), 65 mg cholesterol, 155 mg sodium, 2 g fiber

ORANGE TRUFFLE TART IN CHOCOLATE TART DOUGH

The chocolate dough for this tart is prebaked blind (with no filling).

CHOCOLATE TART DOUGH
- 1¼ cups all-purpose flour
- ½ cup sugar
- ¼ cup unsweetened cocoa
- ¼ teaspoon salt
- 10 tablespoons chilled unsalted butter, cut into ½-inch cubes
- 1 teaspoon vanilla
- 5 to 6 tablespoons ice water

ORANGE TRUFFLE FILLING
- 2 oranges
- 1½ cups heavy whipping cream
- 10 oz. semisweet or bittersweet chocolate
- ¼ cup (½ stick) unsalted butter, cut into small cubes
- Chocolate curls or unsweetened cocoa

❶ In food processor, pulse flour, sugar, cocoa and salt to blend well. Add butter; pulse 15 to 20 times until cubes are about half their original size. Add vanilla to 2 tablespoons of the ice water; pour through feed tube with machine running. Add another 3 to 4 tablespoons ice water, 1 to 2 tablespoons at a time, running machine only when pouring water through tube. Stop while pastry still looks crumbly and dry. With spoon, scoop some dough out of bowl; press in your hand. Turn dough out onto lightly floured surface.

❷ Finish by smearing dough away from you in several strokes with heel of your hand. Fold dough into a ball. Wrap in plastic wrap; let rest in refrigerator 30 to 60 minutes. Roll out dough between 2 pieces of plastic wrap to fit 9-inch tart pan. Peel off top layer of plastic; turn dough into tart pan. Refrigerate 15 to 30 minutes. Put baking sheet in oven; heat to 375°F. Prick dough with fork. Put piece of aluminum foil on top of dough; fill with pie weights. Bake tart shell on baking sheet 20 to 25 minutes. Remove foil and weights. Prick pastry again; bake 5 to 10 minutes or until dough is thoroughly cooked. Remove from oven; cool completely on wire rack.

❸ Scrub oranges under running water. Dry; remove peel in strips with vegetable peeler. In saucepan, bring orange peel and cream to a low boil. Remove from heat; let steep 10 minutes. Meanwhile, chop chocolate into uniform small pieces; put in mixing bowl with butter. Return cream to a simmer; strain over chocolate and butter. Let sit 3 to 5 minutes to melt chocolate. Stir gently with spoon or whisk, taking care not to stir a lot of air into chocolate. Pour filling into tart shell. Refrigerate several hours before serving. After filling has completely cooled, decorate tart with chocolate curls or dust with unsweetened cocoa.

10 servings.

Preparation time: 45 minutes. Ready to serve: 8 hours.

Per serving: 505 calories, 36.5 g total fat (22.5 g saturated fat), 85 mg cholesterol, 85 mg sodium, 2.5 g fiber.

PALMIERS OR PALM LEAVES

Palmiers are best when eaten the day they're made. Before rolling, dust the countertop with sugar instead of flour.

About ¾ cup sugar
½ recipe prepared *Quick Puff Pastry* (page 156)

1. Spread ½ cup of the sugar on countertop.
2. Roll dough to 10x12-inch rectangle. As you work, gently press sugar into both sides of dough with your hands and rolling pin. Use more sugar if needed. Fold each long side twice toward center; adjust corners and edges to keep them square and straight. Fold once more to create long roll of 6 layers.
3. Heat oven to 350°F. Line baking sheet with parchment paper.
4. Sprinkle remaining sugar on countertop. Cut ¼- to ½-inch slices along length of dough. After cutting each cookie, roll it gently in sugar; place on baking sheet, leaving 2 inches between cookies.
5. Bake cookies, one sheet at a time, 25 to 30 minutes or until golden brown. Sugar on bottom of cookies will be lightly caramelized. Transfer to wire rack.

About 2 dozen cookies.

Preparation time: 15 minutes. Ready to serve: 1 hour, 15 minutes.

Per serving: 100 calories, 6 g total fat (3.5 g saturated fat), 15 mg cholesterol, 50 mg sodium, 0 g fib

INDIVIDUAL SPICE BERRY NAPOLEONS

The puff pastry for this recipe is baked with a weight to keep it flat, although it will still be crisp and flaky. You can bake the pastry several hours ahead; store in an airtight container. If necessary, crisp the pastry briefly in a moderate oven for a few minutes.

PASTRY
1/2 recipe prepared *Quick Puff Pastry* (page 156)

BERRIES
4 cups mixed berries, cut into bite-size chunks
2 tablespoons sugar
1/2 teaspoon ground ginger
1/4 teaspoon freshly ground nutmeg
2 tablespoons fruit liqueur such as Grand Marnier, crème de cassis, etc.

SAUCE
1 cup heavy whipping cream
1/4 cup sugar
2 to 3 tablespoons liquid from macerated berries
1/2 teaspoon vanilla

GARNISH
Powdered sugar for dusting (optional)

1. Roll puff pastry into 12x16-inch rectangle. Transfer pastry to flat baking sheet or back of rimmed baking sheet. With pastry wheel, trim away 1/8 inch on all 4 sides; cut dough into 12 equal squares. Refrigerate 20 to 30 minutes.

2. Heat oven to 425°F. Prick pastry squares with fork; cover with rectangular cooling rack (or second cookie sheet). Bake 10 minutes. Reduce oven temperature to 375°F; bake an additional 10 to 20 minutes or until pastry is golden brown and crisp. (If you covered pastry with second cookie sheet, remove it during last 5 to 10 minutes to allow even browning.) Gently remove cooling rack; transfer squares to another rack to cool. When pastry is cool, trim any dark or irregular spots with serrated knife.

3. About 1 hour before serving, prepare berries by tossing in large mixing bowl with 2 tablespoons sugar, ginger, nutmeg and liqueur. Set aside to macerate, stirring occasionally.

4. To make sauce: In mixing bowl, whip cream, 1/4 cup sugar and some berry maceration liquid until it holds soft peaks. Stir in vanilla.

5. To assemble Napoleons: Set aside 6 of the most attractive squares for tops. Put remaining 6 squares on 6 dessert plates. Cover squares with cream sauce. With slotted spoon, scoop berries onto cream; cover with 6 reserved squares. Put dollop of cream sauce on top of each square; dust with powdered sugar. Store in refrigerator.

6 servings.

Preparation time: 25 minutes. Ready to serve: 1 hour, 45 minutes.

Per serving: 530 calories, 36 g total fat (22 g saturated fat), 105 mg cholesterol, 210 mg sodium, 5 g fiber.

FRESH FRUIT TART

Choose fruits of contrasting flavors and colors.

1/2	recipe prepared *Quick Puff Pastry* (page 156)
1	teaspoon cream
1/2	cup jam or jelly
1	recipe *Vanilla Pastry Cream*, chilled (page 158)
3 to 4	cups sliced or cut-up best-quality seasonal fresh fruit

❶ Roll pastry into 8x14-inch rectangle. Trim away 1/8 inch on all 4 sides. Cut 1-inch strip down each long side. Transfer large center piece to baking sheet. Moisten 1 inch of long sides with cold water to act as "glue"; place 1 narrow strip on each side, gently pressing into place. Take care to stretch narrow pieces as little as possible; once they are in place, trim if necessary. To help anchor top edges, make small nicks every 1/4 inch down both long sides with table knife or backside of paring knife. If desired, score tops of side strips with shallow diagonal cuts. Use small brush or your finger to "wash" tops of edges with cream. Refrigerate 15 to 30 minutes.

❷ Heat oven to 425°F. Trim 1/8 inch from both short ends. Prick pastry, including edge strips. Place narrow strip of aluminum foil down center of pastry; pull up edges of foil. Pour in about 1 1/2 cups pie weights. Roll foil over weights so it does not prevent rims from rising. Bake 10 minutes. Reduce oven temperature to 375°F; bake an additional 15 minutes. Remove foil with weights; return pastry to oven an additional 5 to 10 minutes or until center is lightly browned. Transfer to wire rack.

❸ To assemble tart: In small saucepan, stir jam over low heat until melted and smooth. Brush bottom of cooled pastry with jam (this prevents bottom from getting soggy). Spread pastry cream evenly over jam between rims. Place fruit on top of pastry cream randomly or according to color as you wish. Brush more jam on top of fruit as glaze. To serve, cut 2-inch slices across tart. Store in refrigerator.

8 servings.

Preparation time: 15 minutes. Ready to serve: 1 hour, 15 minutes.

Per serving: 415 calories, 20 g total fat (12 g saturated fat), 130 mg cholesterol, 175 mg sodium, 2 g fiber.

VARIATION **Tropical Fruit Tart**
Select fruits such as banana, mango, kiwi, pineapple and papaya. Make Ginger Pastry Cream variation of *Vanilla Pastry Cream* (page 158). Garnish with toasted coconut, if desired.

FRESH PLUM TART WITH GINGERSNAPS IN ALMOND TART DOUGH

This tart makes a great family dessert, and it is the epitome of home cooking —
straightforward and delicious.

ALMOND TART DOUGH

1½ cups all-purpose flour

3 tablespoons sugar

¼ teaspoon salt

½ cup (1 stick) cold unsalted
butter, cut into ½-inch cubes

½ cup coarsely chopped slivered
almonds

4 to 5 tablespoons ice water

FILLING

1½ to 2 lb. fresh plums, halved, pits
removed

⅓ cup sugar (white, brown or a
combination)

⅔ cup gingersnap cookie crumbs
(about 12 cookies)

1 tablespoon butter

1. In food processor, pulse flour, sugar and salt to blend well. Add butter and
almonds; pulse 15 to 20 times until butter pieces are about half their original
size and almonds are in small chunks. Add ice water, 1 to 2 tablespoons at a
time, through feed tube. Run machine only when pouring water through tube;
stop machine while you refill measuring spoon with water. Stop while pastry
still looks crumbly and dry. With spoon, scoop some dough out of bowl; press
in your hand. Turn dough out onto lightly floured surface. Finish by smearing
dough away from you in several strokes with heel of your hand. Fold dough
into a ball. Wrap in plastic wrap; let rest in refrigerator 30 to 60 minutes.

2. Roll out dough to fit 9-inch tart pan; turn dough into pan. Refrigerate 15 to 30
minutes.

3. Put baking sheet in oven; heat to 375°F. Prick dough with fork. Put piece of
aluminum foil on top of dough; fill with pie weights. Bake tart shell on baking
sheet 15 to 20 minutes until edge of tart starts to brown. Remove foil and
weights. Prick pastry again. Bake 5 to 7 minutes to set dough on bottom of pan;
it will lose its raw look and become opaque. Remove tart shell from oven (leave
in baking sheet).

4. Meanwhile, in mixing bowl, toss plums with sugar. Spread gingersnap crumbs
evenly in half-baked tart shell. Spread plums symmetrically on top of
gingersnaps; dot with butter.

5. Return tart to oven. Bake about 50 minutes or until fruit is cooked and pastry is
golden brown. Allow tart to rest at least 30 minutes before serving. Serve plain
or with scoop of ice cream.

8 servings.

Preparation time: 20 minutes. Ready to serve: 3 hours, 40 minutes.

Per serving: 380 calories, 18 g total fat (8.5 g saturated fat), 35 mg cholesterol, 135 mg sodium, 2.5 g fiber.

PROFITEROLES WITH ICE CREAM AND CHOCOLATE CINNAMON SAUCE

Profiterolo, which means "small profit" or "small pleasure," is the French name for a miniature cream puff. Even though the profiterole is small, it is very enjoyable indeed.

SMALL CREAM PUFFS

1 recipe prepared *Cream Puff Pastry* (page 157)

CHOCOLATE CINNAMON SAUCE

2 cups unsweetened cocoa

1 cup sugar

1 teaspoon ground cinnamon

Dash salt

2 cups milk or cream

2 teaspoons vanilla

ICE CREAM

1 quart vanilla ice cream

❶ Heat oven to 375°F. Line baking sheet with parchment paper.

❷ Form cream puffs by piping small rounds through pastry bag fitted with ½-inch plain tip or by dropping dough with spoon. Leave 1 to 2 inches space around each puff. If desired, wet a fingertip and pat down any pointy tops.

❸ Bake one baking sheet at a time 20 to 30 minutes or until puffs are browned and firm. Interiors should remain slightly moist. Transfer to wire rack to cool.

❹ In saucepan, whisk together cocoa, sugar, cinnamon and salt until blended; stir in milk. Stir over low heat until sauce is very warm and smooth. Taste for graininess to make sure sugar has completely dissolved. Simmer 1 minute, stirring slowly.

❺ Remove from heat; stir in vanilla.

❻ Slice cream puffs in half horizontally; arrange 3 bottom halves on each plate. Put 1 small scoop ice cream on each bottom half; top with upper half. Drizzle Chocolate Cinnamon Sauce over each plate; serve.

6 servings.

Preparation time: 25 minutes. Ready to serve: 25 minutes.

Per serving: 585 calories, 25 g total fat (14.5 g saturated fat), 135 mg cholesterol, 235 mg sodium, 10.5 g fiber.

$\mathscr{P}$IES

by Bruce Weinstein and Mark Scarbrough

You do not have to be a master pastry chef to make great pies. All it takes are a few simple ingredients, a couple of basic tools, and a little bit of pie-making strategy. All three factors come together easily ... for classic, down-home, nostalgic and delicious results.

Strawberry Rhubarb Pie, page 174

Pies may be the quintessential American treat, homey and even a little nostalgic. A luscious pie cooling on a window sill? It's our heritage, along with Huck Finn, Andy Griffith and Minnie Pearl. Somehow, word's gotten around that pies are hard to make. Nothing could be further from the truth. Yes, fruit pies are an off-shoot of French tarts. But they're a Yankee strain, cross-bred with a no-nonsense, no-frills, can-do logic. Drop the fancy pastry cream, drop the fussy puff pastry, and voilà — an American classic is born.

No one's exactly sure who made the first pie; no one's even sure who coined the word. Some theorize it's from "magpie," a bird notorious (at least in legend) for hiding trinkets in her nest. More theoretical types suggest pie comes from the Middle English pied, *a word meaning mottled, and so a reference to the filling. What we do know is this: With a few simple tools and a few easy techniques, pies are a snap to make and a pleasure to eat.*

INGREDIENTS

Use only the ingredients called for in the recipe. Measure carefully and read the directions before you do anything — this helps you organize before you begin.

CREAM. To make the best, lightest whipped cream, always use heavy cream just out of the refrigerator. It also helps to chill the bowl and the beaters before using them.

EGGS. Store eggs in the refrigerator but never use them cold. Always let eggs come back to room temperature. Meringues will be higher when the egg whites have come to room temperature; fillings, less likely to break if the yolks aren't cold. If the slightest bit of yolk gets into the egg whites, a meringue won't whip up. To avoid mishaps, don't separate eggs all at once into the mixing bowl — one drop of yolk from the fourth egg will make the whole mixture worthless. Instead, separate the eggs one at a time into a measuring cup or small bowl before transferring them to the larger bowl.

FRUIT. Use only fresh ripe fruit for pies, never canned. Frozen fruit will work in a pinch — but the resulting filling will be wetter and therefore runnier. And there's only one rule for selecting the best fruit: Smell it. If it doesn't smell like anything, it won't taste like any-thing.

FLOUR. Use all-purpose flour in pies, preferably unbleached. Do not use bread flour (the high gluten content will make the dough sticky), cake flour (the high starch content will make the dough brittle), or self-rising flour (the added baking soda and salt will radically change the chemistry of the crust).

TOOLS

After the standard kitchen tools, there are really only three special ones needed to make the perfect pie.

PASTRY CUTTER. This half-moon tool with five to eight blades is perfect for cutting butter or shortening into flour-based crusts. By rocking the blades back and forth in the mixture, and by rotating the bowl slightly with each cut, you can create a tender, flaky crust that's flexible enough to roll out evenly. Some cooks prefer to use two forks for cutting in the butter or shortening. Frankly, we find that technique far more tedious and the results far less rewarding. Forks often leave clumps of fat in the flour, clumps which then do not incorporate into the baked crust.

PIE PLATE. All our recipes call for a 9-inch pie plate. Pie plates are measured on the diameter, from the inside lip straight across. Heat-proof glass pie plates work more efficiently than metal ones. The glass transfers the heat quickly, allowing the crust to set and brown first, thus sealing it against the juicy filling.

PIE WEIGHTS. When you prebake a crust (that is, when you bake it before adding the filling), it needs to be weighted down — otherwise, it may bubble or sag as it heats. Conventional, ceramic pie weights (right) are sold at most gourmet stores. They  are reusable. You may also use 2 cups of dried beans. Afterwards, the beans will not be suitable for cooking and eating, but they may be reserved for future crusts.

TERMS AND TECHNIQUES

Although any crust can be a fearful thing, graham-cracker crusts and chocolate cookie-crusts are really quite easy. It's the "short crusts" (that is, those with a flour and fat combination) that present the most challenges. For great results, follow these tips.

- The first step in making a short crust: Ice water. To make the perfect shortening or butter crust, the water binding the flour and fat must be *very* cold, so that the glutens in the flour don't begin to cohere and the fat doesn't liquefy. Always begin a short crust by setting aside a small bowl of ice water — but strain the ice out before using the water.

- The one rule of thumb: no thumbs at all. The less you handle a short dough, the more tender it will be. Some chefs suggest you use your hands to cut in the butter or shortening, rubbing the fat into the flour with your fingers. Bad idea, because the natural oils on your skin toughen pastry dough considerably. To that end, minimize touching the dough.

- Roll a pie crust on the radius, not the diameter. Rolling a dough edge to edge can lead to mis-shapen pie crusts, ones with jagged peninsulas and inlets. Instead, set the rolling pin down in the middle of the dough and roll out toward the edges, not across the entire piece of dough. Rotate the rolling pin by 10 degrees, and repeat the process, always starting at the middle of the dough and rolling out. And always let your rolling pin do the work — don't press down hard.

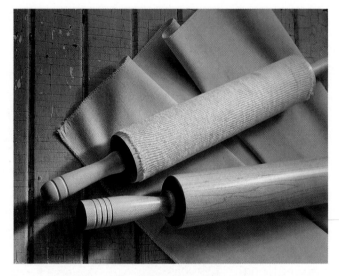

- Roll out a crust between layers of parchment paper. Place a few drops of water on your work surface, then lay a large sheet of parchment paper over them (the water keeps the parchment paper steady). Sprinkle with flour, mound the dough onto it, sprinkle the dough with flour, then top with a second, large sheet of parchment paper. Press down gently to form a disk of dough, then begin rolling out to the desired size. When the dough is the right diameter, remove the top sheet of parchment paper, pick up the bottom sheet with the dough on it, and invert it into the pie plate, using the parchment paper as a shield while you press the dough into place. Finally, peel off the parchment paper and bake or fill as directed.

- Before baking, freeze butter crusts, but not shortening crusts. If a butter-based crust is frozen 10 minutes before it's baked, the butter doesn't instantly melt and cause the crust to sag. Shortening crusts, however, don't need to be frozen first, because freezing does little for vegetable-based shortenings.

TIPS AND INSIGHTS

Remember these tips for easier pie baking

- Position the oven rack correctly. A pie crust should be baked in the bottom third of the oven; a filled pie should be baked in the middle of the oven.

- No drips today, no clean-up tomorrow. Fruit and custard pies bubble, and often drip maddeningly, as they bake. Tempting as it might be, don't put them on a cookie sheet, for the heat circulation will be fundamentally compromised. Instead, lay a small piece of aluminum foil on an oven rack positioned just below the pie.

- Haste makes waste. All pies need to set. Chiffon pies need to go into the freezer for several hours. Fruit pies need to cool on a wire rack 30 minutes; if any pie is cut too soon, it will run, crumble and collapse.

- Use only the freshest of ingredients — and that includes the cookies and crackers you use in those types of crusts!

STRAWBERRY RHUBARB PIE

This sweet and tart pie is heavenly when served warm with homemade vanilla ice cream. A combination of tapioca and flour keeps the filling firm without making it too gelatinous. Fresh strawberries are a must, but you can substitute frozen rhubarb in a pinch. The top "crust" is an American classic with a twist: An oat topping spiked with ginger. This pie is also pictured on pages 168-169.

CRUST
1 baked 9-inch Shortening Crust (page 177), cooled

FILLING
1¼ cups sugar

3 tablespoons all-purpose flour

2 tablespoons instant tapioca pearls

½ teaspoon salt

2 cups fresh strawberries, hulled, thickly sliced

2 cups fresh rhubarb, cut into 1-inch slices or frozen, thawed

2 tablespoons unsalted butter, at room temperature

TOPPING
½ cup (1 stick) unsalted butter, melted, at room temperature

½ cup all-purpose flour

½ cup quick cooking oats, lightly toasted

½ cup packed light brown sugar

¼ cup sugar

¼ cup chopped walnuts

1½ teaspoons ground ginger

❶ Heat oven to 350°F.

❷ In large bowl, stir 1¼ cups sugar, 3 tablespoons flour, tapioca and salt until combined. Add strawberries and rhubarb; toss to coat well. Pour mixture into crust; dot with 2 tablespoons butter. Set aside 10 minutes.

❸ In large bowl, mix melted butter, ½ cup flour, oats, brown sugar, ¼ cup sugar, walnuts and ginger with fork until combined. Crumble over pie.

❹ Bake about 40 minutes or until filling bubbles. Cool on wire rack; store, covered, at room temperature up to 4 days.

8 servings.

Preparation time: 20 minutes. Ready to serve: 2 hours, 35 minutes.

Per serving: 575 calories, 27. 5 g total fat (11. 5 g saturated fat), 40 mg cholesterol, 445 mg sodium, 3 g fiber.

174

LEMON CHESS PIE

This pie really doesn't need anything else — except maybe candied violets or candied rose petals for garnish, if you have them.

CRUST
1 baked 9-inch Shortening Crust (page 177), cooled

FILLING
1¼ cups sugar

6 tablespoons unsalted butter, at room temperature

3 eggs plus 2 egg yolks, at room temperature, well beaten

¼ cup buttermilk (whole, low-fat or nonfat)

2 tablespoons cornmeal

1 tablespoon grated lemon peel

¼ cup lemon juice

½ teaspoon salt

1. Heat oven to 350°F.

2. In large bowl, beat sugar and butter at medium speed until thick and pale yellow, about 5 minutes. Stir in eggs and egg yolks just until combined. Stir in buttermilk, cornmeal, lemon peel, lemon juice and salt until combined; pour into crust.

3. Bake about 40 minutes or until set. Cool; refrigerate, covered, up to 3 days.

8 servings.

Preparation time: 15 minutes. Ready to serve: 2 hours, 22 minutes.

Per serving: 400 calories, 22. 5 g total fat (9 g saturated fat), 160 mg cholesterol, 470 mg sodium, . 5 g fiber.

APPLE CRANBERRY CRUMB PIE

The secret to a good apple pie is, well, the apples! Choose firm, crisp ones, like McIntosh, Granny Smith or Rome.

BUTTER CRUST

1¼ cups all-purpose flour, plus additional for dusting

1 teaspoon sugar

1 teaspoon salt

6 tablespoons unsalted butter, cut into 1-inch chunks and very cold

2 tablespoons margarine, cut into 1-inch chunks and very cold

4 to 5 tablespoons ice water

FILLING

½ cup sugar

2 tablespoons all-purpose flour

½ teaspoon ground cinnamon

4 large tart apples (about 2 lb.), peeled, cored, thinly sliced and placed in acidulated water

1 cup dried cranberries

Juice of 1 lemon

CRUMB TOPPING

1½ cups all-purpose flour

¼ cup packed light brown sugar

¼ cup pure maple syrup

¼ cup finely chopped walnuts

6 tablespoons unsalted butter, melted

❶ Heat oven to 400°F. In large bowl, stir 1¼ cups of the flour, 1 teaspoon sugar and salt until combined. Using pastry blender, cut in 6 tablespoons butter and margarine until mixture crumbles. With fork, stir in ice water, 1 tablespoon at a time, just until dough forms. Gather dough into ball; wrap in plastic wrap. Refrigerate 30 minutes. Lay 1 large sheet parchment paper on work surface; flour lightly. Place unwrapped, chilled dough on parchment paper. Flour dough lightly; cover with second sheet of parchment paper. Press dough into a round; roll into 10-inch round. Transfer to 9-inch pie plate; remove second sheet of parchment paper. Trim and crimp edges. Repeatedly prick bottom and sides with fork. Line crust with aluminum foil; fill with pie weights or dried beans. Freeze 10 minutes; bake 8 minutes. Remove foil and pie weights; cool on wire rack. Crust can be made 1 day ahead and kept, covered, at room temperature.

❷ Reduce oven temperature to 350°F. In large bowl, stir ½ cup sugar, 2 tablespoons flour, and cinnamon until combined. Toss apple slices, cranberries and lemon juice in mixture to coat. Pile into crust.

❸ In medium bowl, stir 1½ cups flour, brown sugar, maple syrup, walnuts and 6 tablespoons butter until stiff dough forms. Crumble evenly over filling; lightly press in place. Bake about 45 minutes or until top is lightly brown and juices bubble at edges. Cool on wire rack; store, covered, at room temperature up to 3 days.

8 servings.

Preparation time: 35 minutes. Ready to serve: 3 hours, 48 minutes.

Per serving: 575 calories, 23 g total fat (11. 5 g saturated fat), 45 mg cholesterol, 340 mg sodium, 5 g fiber.

BURNT SUGAR PIE

This is an old Southern classic.

SHORTENING CRUST
- 1 cup all-purpose flour, plus additional for dusting
- 1 teaspoon salt
- 1/3 cup plus 1 tablespoon shortening
- 1 teaspoon cider vinegar
- 3 to 4 tablespoons ice water

FILLING
- 3 tablespoons cornstarch
- 1 1/2 tablespoons all-purpose flour
- 1/2 teaspoon salt
- 2 cups sugar
- 3 egg yolks, at room temperature, lightly beaten
- 2 2/3 cups milk (whole or low-fat, but not nonfat)
- 2 tablespoons unsalted butter
- 2 teaspoons vanilla

MERINGUE
- 6 egg whites, at room temperature
- 1/4 cup sugar
- 1 teaspoon cream of tartar

❶ Heat oven to 425°F. In large bowl, stir 1 cup of the flour and 1 teaspoon salt until combined. Using pastry blender, cut shortening into mixture until mixture crumbles. Add vinegar, then ice water 1 tablespoon at a time, stirring with fork until dough sticks together. Turn out onto large piece of floured parchment paper. Sprinkle with flour; top with second sheet of parchment paper. Roll to 11-inch round; transfer to 9-inch pie plate, peeling back parchment paper. Trim and crimp edges. Repeatedly prick bottom and sides with fork. Line dough with aluminum foil; fill with pie weights or dried beans. Bake 10 minutes or until flaky and light brown. Cool on wire rack. Crust can be made ahead 1 day and kept, covered, at room temperature. Reduce oven temperature to 375°F. In large bowl, whisk together cornstarch, 1 1/2 tablespoons flour, 1/2 teaspoon salt and 1/2 cup of the sugar until well combined. Whisk in egg yolks and 1/3 cup of the milk until smooth. Set aside.

❷ In large saucepan, bring remaining 2 1/3 cups milk to a simmer; maintain milk's temperature while caramelizing sugar. In heavy skillet, preferably cast iron, caramelize remaining 1 1/2 cups sugar over medium-high heat. Stir until sugar melts, then cook without stirring until dark brown. Reduce heat to medium; slowly pour caramelized sugar into warm milk mixture, stirring constantly. Be careful — mixture will boil. Stir down boil until smooth, about 3 minutes. When smooth, whisk in egg yolk mixture. Cook over low heat, stirring constantly, about 3 minutes or just until thickened. Remove from heat; stir in butter and vanilla. Pour into crust. In large bowl, beat egg whites at high speed until frothy. Beat in 1/4 cup sugar and cream of tartar until stiff peaks form. Spoon onto hot custard, sealing meringue against edges of crust with rubber spatula. Bake about 10 minutes or until meringue browns.

8 servings.

Preparation time: 60 minutes. Ready to serve: 4 hours. **Per serving: 495 calories, 18 g total fat (6. 5 g saturated fat), 100 mg cholesterol, 520 mg sodium, . 5 g fiber.**

COCONUT CREME BRULEE PIE

This rich pie is made from an egg custard laced with coconut. After the pie bakes, put it under the broiler to create a "crème brûlée" finish. To prevent the crust from burning, wrap a 1-inch sheet of aluminum foil around the crust's edges before placing the pie under the broiler.

CRUST
- 1 baked 9-inch Butter Crust (page 176), doubled, cooled

FILLING
- 1 cup sweetened shredded coconut
- 1 (14-oz.) coconut milk
- 1 cup milk (whole, low-fat or nonfat)
- ½ cup sugar
- 4 eggs, at room temperature, lightly beaten
- 1 teaspoon vanilla
- ½ teaspoon salt

TOPPING
- ¼ cup packed light brown sugar
- ⅓ cup sweetened shredded coconut

1. Heat oven to 325°F. Press dough into 6 (4½-inch) pie plates. Sprinkle ¼ cup coconut evenly over each crust.

2. In large bowl, stir together coconut milk, milk and sugar until smooth. Stir in eggs, vanilla and salt. Pour mixture evenly over coconut.

3. Bake about 45 minutes or until knife inserted into center of each filling comes out clean. Cool completely on wire rack.

4. Position oven rack 4 inches from broiler; heat broiler. In medium bowl, mix brown sugar and ⅓ cup coconut; sprinkle mixture evenly over custard. Broil 1 minute or until sugar caramelizes.

5. Serve immediately or refrigerate, covered, up to 4 days.

8 servings.

Preparation time: 15 minutes. Ready to serve: 2 hours, 45 minutes.

Per serving: 470 calories, 30 g total fat (20 g saturated fat), 135 mg cholesterol, 570 mg sodium, 1 g fiber.

NESSELRODE PIE

Count Nesselrode was a 19th century Russian diplomat, now legendary for his prodigious appetite. His personal chef created this luscious frozen chestnut custard, laced with glacéd fruits. (We've even added chocolate chips, outdoing the old Count.)

GRAHAM CRACKER CRUST
- 1⅓ cups graham cracker crumbs
- ⅓ cup sugar
- ⅓ cup unsalted butter, melted and cooled

FILLING
- 2 egg yolks, at room temperature
- ⅓ cup sugar
- 1½ cups milk (whole or low-fat, but not nonfat)
- 1 (¼-oz.) envelope unflavored gelatin, softened 10 minutes in ¼ cup dark rum
- 1 cup chestnut puree
- 1 cup whipping cream
- 2 tablespoons powdered sugar
- 1 teaspoon vanilla
- ½ cup plus 2 tablespoons chopped glacéd fruit (such as pineapple, cherries or papaya)
- ½ cup plus 2 tablespoons semisweet chocolate chips

1 Heat oven to 350°F. In large bowl, mix graham cracker crumbs, ⅓ cup sugar and butter until uniform. Press gently into bottom and up sides of 9-inch pie plate. Bake 5 minutes; cool on wire rack.

2 In medium bowl, whisk yolks and ⅓ cup sugar until thick and pale yellow, about 5 minutes. In saucepan, heat milk to a simmer over low heat. Whisk warm milk into egg yolk mixture; return to saucepan. Raise heat to medium-low; cook, stirring constantly, until just thick enough to coat back of wooden spoon, about 1 minute. Remove from heat and whisk in softened gelatin and rum; whisk in chestnut puree until smooth. Using fine-mesh sieve, strain into clean, large bowl, pushing mixture through sieve with back of wooden spoon. Refrigerate, uncovered, until cool and slightly set, about 1 hour.

3 In large bowl, whip cream, powdered sugar and vanilla at medium speed until stiff. Fold whipped cream, ½ cup of the glacéd fruit and ½ cup of the chocolate chips into chilled chestnut cream. Return to refrigerator until mixture can hold its shape without flattening out on spoon, about 10 minutes. Mound chestnut cream in crust; sprinkle with remaining 2 tablespoons glacéd fruit and chocolate chips. Freeze at least 4 hours.

8 servings.

Preparation time: 40 minutes. Ready to serve: 5 hours, 4 minutes.

Per serving: 465 calories, 25 g total fat (14. 5 g saturated fat), 110 mg cholesterol, 150 mg sodium, 2 g fiber.

HEATH BAR MILE HIGH CHOCOLATE CREAM PIE

Although this easy chocolate pie is rich enough to satisfy the chocolate lover in all of us, we've left the cream out of the filling, making it denser but also lighter. This pie is actually best the second day, after the flavors have had a chance to meld and ripen.

CRUST
1 baked 9-inch Shortening Crust (page 177), cooled

FILLING
3 oz. unsweetened chocolate, chopped
2 oz. bittersweet or semisweet chocolate, chopped
1 cup sugar
3 tablespoons cornstarch
1/2 teaspoon salt
3 cups milk (whole or low-fat, but not nonfat)

3 egg yolks, lightly beaten
2 tablespoons unsalted butter, at room temperature
1 teaspoon gold or white rum
1 teaspoon vanilla

TOPPING
1 cup whipping cream, chilled
2 tablespoons powdered sugar
3 (1. 3-oz.) toffee candy bars, chopped
Grated chocolate for garnish

1. Heat oven to 350°F.

2. In top of double boiler or bowl that fits snugly over small pot of simmering water, melt unsweetened and bittersweet chocolates. Stir until smooth; remove from heat.

3. In large saucepan, stir sugar, cornstarch and salt until combined; whisk in milk in thin stream. Bring to a simmer over medium heat, whisking constantly. Whisk 1 cup hot mixture into egg yolks; whisk egg yolk mixture back into saucepan. Cook 1 minute over low heat, stirring constantly. Remove from heat; whisk in melted chocolates, butter, rum and vanilla until smooth. Set aside 10 minutes; pour into crust. Cool; refrigerate, covered with plastic wrap, 3 hours or overnight.

4. In large bowl, whip cream and powdered sugar with electric mixer at high speed until soft peaks form. Fold in candy bars; spoon decoratively into pie. Sprinkle with grated chocolate. Refrigerate, covered, up to 3 days.

8 servings.

Preparation time: 35 minutes. Ready to serve: 3 hours, 35 minutes.

Per serving: 630 calories, 40. 5 g total fat (20. 5 g saturated fat), 150 mg cholesterol, 525 mg sodium, 2. 5 g fiber.

RASPBERRY MINT CHIFFON PIE

A chiffon pie, made with whipping cream and gelatin, has long been a favorite of luncheons and church buffets. This berry-laced, minty version makes a refreshing summer treat.

CRUST

1   unbaked 9-inch Chocolate Crumb Crust (page 185)

FILLING

2   cups fresh raspberries
1   cup whipping cream
3   pasteurized eggs, at room temperature, separated
2/3 cup plus 3 tablespoons sugar
1   (1/4-oz.) pkg. unflavored gelatin, softened 10 minutes with 1/4 cup cranberry juice
1   tablespoon raspberry liqueur (optional)
1/2 teaspoon mint extract

1. Heat oven to 350°F. Freeze crust 10 minutes; bake 8 minutes. Cool on wire rack.

2. Meanwhile, using back of wooden spoon, press raspberries through fine-mesh sieve into medium bowl, removing seeds. Set puree aside. In large saucepan, bring cream to a simmer. Immediately remove from heat; set aside.

3. In large bowl, beat egg yolks and 2/3 cup of the sugar at medium speed until thick and pale yellow. Slowly pour warm cream into beaten egg yolk mixture; return to saucepan over low heat. Stir constantly until mixture coats back of wooden spoon, about 3 minutes. Do not boil. If egg yolks curdle, strain through fine-mesh sieve into large clean bowl.

4. Stir softened gelatin and cranberry juice into cream mixture; stir in raspberry puree, liqueur and mint extract. Refrigerate until mixture thickens slightly, about 15 minutes.

5. In large bowl, beat egg whites at high speed until frothy. Add remaining 3 tablespoons sugar. Continue beating until stiff peaks form; fold into raspberry mixture. Return to refrigerator about 20 minutes or until mixture can hold its shape without flattening out on spoon. Spread into crust; refrigerate 3 hours before serving. Refrigerate, covered, up to 3 days.

8 servings.

Preparation time: 30 minutes. Ready to serve: 1 hour, 48 minutes.

Per serving: 410 calories, 22 g total fat (12 g saturated fat), 130 mg cholesterol, 190 mg sodium, 3 g fiber.

RAISIN WALNUT GINGER PIE

This modern take on mincemeat pie is, of course, lighter — but it's sweeter too.
The raisins melt a bit, creating a dense, thick filling that's even better the next day.
Serve this rich pie with chocolate, maple or rum raisin ice cream.

CRUST
1   baked 9-inch Butter Crust (page 176), cooled

FILLING
1/4   cup (1/2 stick) unsalted butter, at room temperature
1/2   cup packed dark brown sugar
3   eggs, at room temperature
1/2   cup dark corn syrup
1/2   cup light corn syrup
2   teaspoons vanilla
1/2   teaspoon salt
1   cup raisins
1 1/4   cups chopped walnuts
1/2   cup chopped crystallized ginger

1 Heat oven to 350°F.

2 In large bowl, beat butter and brown sugar at medium speed until pale brown and thick. Beat in eggs, one at a time; beat in dark and light corn syrups, vanilla and salt, scraping down sides of bowl as necessary. Stir in raisins, walnuts and ginger.

3 Pour into crust. Bake about 60 minutes or just until filling is set and middle jiggles only slightly when pie is shaken. Cool on wire rack; store, covered, at room temperature up to 4 days.

8 servings.

Preparation time: 15 minutes. Ready to serve: 2 hours, 45 minutes.

Per serving: 635 calories, 31 g total fat (11 g saturated fat), 120 mg cholesterol, 590 mg sodium, 2. 5 g fiber.

FROZEN MUD PIE

This easy, no-bake pie is like a chocolate sundae in a cookie crust.

CHOCOLATE CRUMB CRUST
35	chocolate wafer cookies
2	tablespoons sugar
5	tablespoons unsalted butter, melted

FILLING
1	pint chocolate ice cream, softened
3/4	cup hot fudge sauce, melted, at room temperature
1	pint coffee ice cream, softened
1/4	cup caramel sauce, melted, at room temperature

TOPPING
1 1/2	cups whipping cream
3	tablespoons powdered sugar
3	tablespoons unsweetened cocoa
1	teaspoon vanilla

1. In food processor, grind cookies and sugar until pulverized. Pour butter through feed tube; process until incorporated. Spread mixture evenly into bottom and up sides of 9-inch pie plate. Freeze 1 hour. Crust can be made ahead; store in freezer up to 1 week.

2. Spoon chocolate ice cream into crust. Spread gently with rubber spatula — do not press down. Cover with 1/2 cup of the hot fudge sauce; spoon on coffee ice cream, covering hot fudge. Drizzle with caramel sauce. Freeze 1 hour.

3. In medium bowl, whip cream, powdered sugar, cocoa and vanilla at medium speed until soft peaks form. Spread evenly over pie. Drizzle remaining 1/4 cup hot fudge sauce over cream. Return to freezer at least 2 hours.

8 servings.

Preparation time: 25 minutes. Ready to serve: 4 hours, 25 minutes.

Per serving: 615 calories, 36. 5 g total fat (20. 5 g saturated fat), 95 mg cholesterol, 295 mg sodium, 2 g fiber

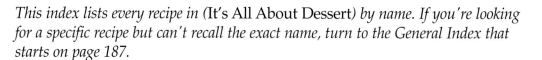

RECIPE INDEX

This index lists every recipe in (It's All About Dessert) *by name. If you're looking for a specific recipe but can't recall the exact name, turn to the General Index that starts on page 187.*

GENERAL INDEX

There are several ways to use this helpful index. First — you can find recipes by name. If you don't know a recipe's specific name but recall a main ingredient, look under that heading and all the related recipes will be listed; scan for the recipe you want. Finally — you can use this general index to find a summary of the recipes in each chapter of the book (bars & brownies, fruite desserts, pies, etc.).

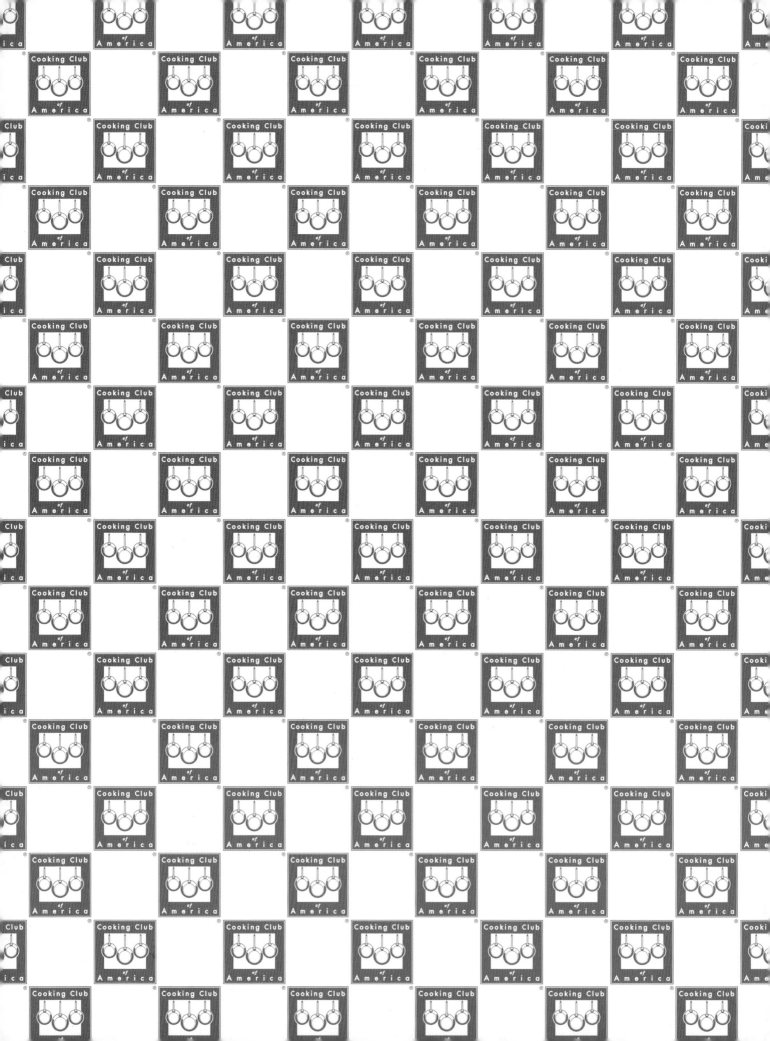